COURSEWORK IN A LEVEL LITERATURE

GW00888615

Peter Buckroyd and Jane Ogborn

Hodder & Stoughton
LONDON SYDNEY AUCKLAND

For
Roy Hopwood
with love and gratitude

British Library Cataloguing in Publication Data:
Buckroyd, Peter
  Coursework in A level and AS English literature.
  I. Title   II. Ogborn, Jane
  820.71

  ISBN 0-340-56191-2

First published 1992

Typeset by Litho Link Ltd, Welshpool, Powys, Wales.
Printed in Great Britain for the educational publishing division of Hodder and Stoughton Ltd, Mill Road, Dunton Green, Sevenoaks, Kent by St Edmundsbury Press Ltd.

CONTENTS

1

INTRODUCTION

—

This book is designed for several purposes. First of all, it attempts to gather together the experience of two people who have been involved from the very beginning with the first freely available part-coursework A level syllabus in English Literature, now the Associated Examining Board's 660 syllabus, officially entitled English (Literature – Alternative). Peter Buckroyd was the first Chief Examiner and Chief Moderator of the syllabus and Jane Ogborn taught the syllabus for ten years, from the beginning of the pilot scheme; she is now a Moderator.

The timing of the book is significant for two reasons. It has become clear that just at the time when AEB 660 is experiencing very rapid growth, it is also becoming impossible with LMS for the Board to continue to insist that all centres entering candidates for this syllabus *must* send one representative to each termly Consortium meeting. Our experience has been that teachers value enormously these termly meetings, run by their Moderator, for it is not just the opportunity for standardisation of pieces of work, but also the forum for discussion about methodologies, problems and approaches. The AEB will be continuing to hold these termly Consortium meetings, but the need now also arises for some fuller written guidance about the course and about its assessment than is available from the Board's 'Notes for Guidance'. Thus this book is published in conjunction with the AEB for the purpose of supplementing the kind of sharing and training which takes place at the Consortium meetings. From 1992 the final moderation of coursework will be either postal moderation or consensus moderation. Thus it seems important for those centres who opt for postal moderation that some fuller guidance should be available.

This book contains guidance about course planning and task setting, based on the syllabus requirements of AEB 660. It also contains a number of examples of students' work with commentaries, drawn from recent 660 coursework. However, it is hoped that this book may appeal not only to teachers embarking on AEB 660, but also to those under-taking coursework with other Boards, and to those considering introducing coursework at AS and A level. For this reason, a grade has been suggested for each student outcome as well as a mark. The mark follows the scheme of assessment for AEB 660, but it must be emphasised that the judgements are those of the authors and not the official marks or grades given by an examination board.

The second reason why the timing of this book is significant is because, at a time of A and AS rationalisation, when most of the Boards have recently introduced more extensive coursework provision than has been the case in the past, the government is proposing to reduce the coursework component of any syllabus to 20% of the available credit. Professor Higginson's proposal (in his report, *Advancing A Levels* (1988)), that all A level syllabuses, whatever the subject, should contain a *minimum* of 20% coursework was a radical one, and for the reasons given below, very much to be welcomed. The authors, and teachers currently teaching the AEB 660 syllabus (which has 50% coursework) deplore the transformation of this proposal into a reduction to a *maximum* of 20% coursework at A Level, again whatever the subject being examined. The decision appears to indicate ignorance of the value of coursework as part of a whole system of assessment, and a lack of understanding of the contribution which coursework can make to a student's development:

- **coursework has an influence on curriculum planning and development**
  It operates more dynamically and flexibly on the classroom situation than a terminal examination can. In order to ensure that students are being offered adequate opportunities to fulfil the syllabus objectives, teachers must plan their course carefully.

- **coursework offers students opportunities for active engagement with the assessment process**
  Successful peformance in coursework is closely related to three factors:
  - the nature of the tasks set;
  - the students' understanding of the criteria by which they will be assessed;
  - the use which is made of the opportunity it offers for dialogue between teacher and student in the course of producing the work.

- **coursework offers students the opportunity to negotiate tasks, set their own goals and develop independence**
  In a terminal examination a candidate must always produce answers to questions and problems posed by someone else.

- **coursework can provide, evidence of the processes involved in carrying out an activity, as well as delivering final products**

Such processes may include drafts of a poem, stages in a design project, the progress of an investigation, a log of a collaborative activity.

- **coursework allows students time to demonstrate skills and abilities**
It can give them time to think, plan in advance, experiment, make mistakes and start again. It shifts the emphasis from the quick final product to a considered, planned response to a problem.

- **coursework can show evidence of original research, wider reading, the ability to sustain work over a period, and at some length**
These qualities are virtually impossible to demonstrate in a conventional terminal examination.

- **the same piece of written coursework can be used for summative as well as formative purposes**
Once completed, it marks a stage in the student's development; it can also become an element of the final folder of evidence which will be reassessed at the end of the course of study. An externally assessed terminal examination obviously provides material for summative purposes only.

Originally, AEB 660 was planned so that the elements of terminal examination and coursework were complementary, and each of the three papers tested different skills. The coursework provides positive opportunities to assess a student's breadth and depth of reading, and the range of her or his responses, but it seems unlikely that these can continue to be offered adequately if that component of the examination is to be reduced to only 20%.

In presenting student outcomes in this book, the authors have typed those pieces which were originally handwritten, but have not otherwise changed them. Readers will therefore encounter technical errors in the written outcomes; these errors are the students', rather than the authors', editors' or printers'! The pieces were not 'corrected', so as to provoke further reflection and discussion in relation to the assessment criteria.

The writers are most grateful to the following who have helped to make this book possible: Glenn Robinson; the current Chief Moderator of AEB 660, Dr Bernard T. Harrison; Moderators Gwen Evans and Sue Hackman for sending interesting and lively coursework to the writers, some of which has been included in the book; and the English departments of all the schools and colleges which have provided material for inclusion, among which are: Francis Holland School, Reigate Sixth Form College, Mascalls School, Worthing Sixth Form College, Francis Combe School, Stevenage College of Further Education, Kings Langley School, St Bede's School, Enfield County School, Gordano School, Collyer's Sixth Form College, Varndean Sixth Form College.

2

CONSTRUCTING A COURSE

—

Teachers embarking on teaching AEB 660 for the first time are instructed to contact their Moderator with information about their choice of coursework texts.

This requirement, apparently a part of the Board's organisational system, has a number of extremely important implications for departmental decision-making and whole course planning. It is not the same as just choosing which books you are going to teach from the list in a more traditional syllabus. Whatever syllabus you are working with, your course needs to be constructed within the framework of the guidance given by the Board, and the syllabus Aims and Objectives. Here are the materials provided by the AEB for 660 (these are the notes for guidance at the time of going to print; they are, however, regularly updated):

1993 EXAMINATION

ENGLISH (*Literature – Alternative***) – 660***   (**Available in June only*)
SYLLABUS III – ADVANCED LEVEL Two written papers, one of 2½ hours and one of 3¼ hours, together with a course-work folder including an extended essay

---

This syllabus incorporates the agreed Inter-Board English Common Core as shown in the booklet *Common Cores at Advanced Level*, copies of which may be obtained from the Board's Publications Department.

Centres wishing to enter candidates for this syllabus must meet the following requirements *before* commencing the course:

i Register as an AEB examination centre;

ii Obtain the approval in writing of The Secretary General (A1) to join a local consortium. Please note that entries cannot be accepted unless a moderator has been appointed to serve a viable group of centres in the region;

iii A moderation fee is payable for each candidate to meet the additional cost of this examination.

Aims

A course based on this syllabus should enable the following to be achieved:

1 appreciation of the wide variety of response which literature evokes;
2 exploration of texts in order to discover fresh insights;
3 understanding of themselves and others;
4 reflection on what has been read;
5 an awareness of ambiguities and an expression of this awareness, where necessary;
6 development of new uses of language in order to articulate perceptions, understandings and insights;
7 completion of projects, in which the choice of topics and the motivation come largely from the students themselves;
8 sensitivity to signs of mood and feeling;
9 interaction with works written for a different kind of society and in a different idiom from the student's own;
10 response in formats other than the traditional discursive or critical essay.

Not all these aims are readily translatable into the assessment objectives which follow.

Assessment Objectives

The examination will assess a candidate's ability to:

1 show first-hand knowledge of a text and, where appropriate, of the personal and historical circumstances in which it was written;
2 see meanings beneath the surface of a text;
3 understand the nature and interplay of characters;
4 show appreciation of an author's style;
5 make a well-considered personal response to a text;
6 show how texts excite emotions in readers or audiences;
7 make interested and informed conjectures, when asked, about the intentions of a writer;
8 sustain a wide reading of an author or of a number of writings on the same theme or in one genre;
9 explore works written for a different kind of society and in a different idiom from the candidate's own;
10 write effectively, and appropriately, in response to texts studied.

Paper 1 will test all Objectives except 1 and 8; Paper 2 and the coursework will test all Objectives.

With effect from the June 1990 examination the Coursework element of 660 will be worth 50% of the total examination. The total marks for the Coursework will be 180, made up as follows:

>   8 units of between 800 and 1200 words – 15 marks each
>   1 extended essay of about 3000 words – 60 marks

The contents and assembly of Coursework folders:

1 Centres must choose a minimum of six texts other than those prescribed in

Paper 2, including at least one Shakespeare play, the poetry of one or more writers, or poetry exploring chosen themes, and a work of non-fiction.

2 Each candidate's folder will contain 8 pieces of work which should be between 800 and 1200 words but work outside these parameters will not be penalised on length alone. The Moderator will look for evidence that each of the chosen texts has been studied.

3 The folder will also contain one extended essay of about 3000 words on a broader basis than a single text. Please note that the title of the extended essay has to be approved by the Moderator before commencement. In the Board's experience, candidates are often tempted to choose over-ambitious titles and it is therefore in their interest to have the topic approved by the Moderator before they start work. Your Moderator will, therefore, probably ask for titles of extended essays to be submitted to him/her before the end of the summer term.

4 It is recommended that a bibliography should be attached to the extended essay where this is appropriate to the subject.

5 The pieces of work must be filed in chronological order and listed on the CIS sheet supplied by the Board.

6 Each piece must be dated, with an explanation of the conditions under which it was produced, clearly written at the top of the first page. Failure to comply with this regulation may result in work not being accepted for assessment.

7 Marks awarded for a centre's candidates should be entered on the CMS sheet supplied by the Board. The CMS should be completed and available to the Moderator in advance of the final moderation meeting.

8 Revised work may be included but once a piece of work has been submitted for formal assessment it may not be further revised.

9 The selection of work is to be determined by the teacher and the candidate in consultation. However, in the unlikely event of any disagreement, the candidate's choice should take precedence.

10 The aggregate mark for each folder is reached by the adding together all marks for work included in the folder.

N.B. Candidates must submit a folder and take both written papers in order to quality for a result. Incomplete folders will be assessed on a pro-rata basis.

The Moderators' responsibilities

Your Moderator's ultimate responsibility is to recommend to the Board a final assessment of coursework folders produced for each candidate in the consortium. To this end he/she will:

a Attend AEB workshops, one per term. Approve, offer advice on, and reject, if necessary, texts chosen for study as Coursework and topics chosen for the extended essay.

b Assist in the training of members of the consortium in the assessment of Coursework.

c Conduct agreement trials to ensure consistency and reliability of marking.

d Sample Coursework assessments from schools and colleges.

Since all teachers will be responsible for some marking which will form part of the final assessment, it is hoped that every effort will be made to ensure at least broad comparability of marking standards between markers at each centre and preferably between all markers in each consortium. Considerable attention will be devoted to this in workshop sessions and it is important that comparability should be achieved before the Moderator makes a final review of the total coursework marks awarded. Each marker will be required to supply a sample of marked folders for review by the Moderator. Folders should be assembled, collated and marked by Easter so that they may be moderated at the beginning of the summer term. Although moderation will be done by sampling, all folders should be available for the consortium moderation. They should be regarded as the property of the Head of Department on behalf of the Board, from the date of the examination until 31st October. This should enable the Board to gain access to them during that period if necessary. There is the opportunity at the end of the moderation process for representatives of centres to meet with the Moderator.

A centre's choice of coursework texts can be determined by many factors:

- teachers' preferences and enthusiasms
- teachers' knowledge of their students, and their sense of what they will find of interest
- teachers' knowledge of the strengths of the colleagues with whom they will be sharing the teaching
- the constraints on resources
- the contents of the stock cupboard.

These are all valid reasons for choosing one text rather than another. But the course as a whole will only work well if these choices are also informed by the Aims and Objectives of the 660 syllabus, and by the department's own rationale for offering an A level literature course, and for choosing 660 as its vehicle.

The syllabus Aims refer to many qualities which such a course should allow students to develop. These are powers of:

- appreciation
- exploration
- understanding
- reflection.

These qualities are to be exercised through the study of texts written in different societies, and in different idioms. Students should be enabled to develop as users of language, and to articulate their responses in a variety of formats, and they should undertake largely original, self-motivated projects.

These Aims set out a curriculum agenda. In the same way, the Assessment Objectives indicate the skills which students should be enabled to exercise and develop during the course. Not only will they be assessed on their firsthand knowledge of texts (Objective 1), on the effectiveness of their written responses (10) and on their ability to sustain wide reading (8); they must also demonstrate their ability to look beneath the surface of texts (2, 3, 6), to comment on features of form and style, as well as on content and ideas (4, 9), to explore and hypothesise (7) and to articulate a well-considered personal response (5). Here we have the guidelines for the course's programme of study.

The question which teachers therefore need to ask themselves is not:

- Which texts would we like to read with this group?

nor even:

- Which texts would this group like to read?

but rather:

- Which texts could we propose for study which would enable students to develop and demonstrate these qualities and skills?

and also:

- How would the texts which we propose to choose (because of our preferences, our colleagues' strengths, the limitations of our current capitation and the contents of our stock cupboard) contribute to a course in which students will be enabled to develop and demonstrate these qualities and skills?

AEB 660 demands a fundamental shift of thinking on the part of A level teachers away from:

- What does this group of students need to know for this examination that we can teach them?

to:

- How can we enable this group of students to develop as readers and writers, and to demonstrate their knowledge, skills and understanding effectively?

This shift in thinking will not necessarily alter a centre's original choice of texts. It ought, however, to have a fundamental effect on the ways they are approached, and on the work which results.

A UNIFIED COURSE

Teachers are sometimes surprised by a Moderator's request for a list of the set books which have been chosen, as well as for a list of their coursework texts. Apart from permitting the checking of possible rubric infringements at final moderation, this information also gives some idea of whether or not the whole course, as planned by the centre, has an internal coherence of its own.

This coherence can be achieved in a variety of different ways, partly through the choice of texts and partly through the approaches to them.

There is always a serious temptation, when centres embark on AEB 660 for the first time, for teachers to perceive the coursework component as disproportionately important. Of course, it is probably the reason why they have changed from their current syllabus, and it is quite understandable that the freedom which the coursework allows them may monopolise the available time and energy as a result. Nevertheless, teachers must remember that even though the coursework component is now worth 50% of the final marks, the other 50% is still earned from end-of-course examinations, which also need thorough preparation.

Consequently, in planning their course as a whole, teachers need to work out how to combine the coursework and the examination preparation in ways which make sense for students. These ways also need to enable them to develop skills in the context of coursework which they can transfer effectively to a terminal examination situation. The need for this dual focus must be appreciated when planning the two-year course:

Examination	+	**Coursework**

Paper 1: Comprehension and
Practical Criticism

+ Paper 3: Six coursework texts

+ Paper 2: Four Set Books

Although the components are set out separately here, it might be more helpful to envisage two-way traffic between them, not based on shared texts, but arising out of shared aims and methodologies. These are the key questions to be asked in connection with each separate component:

Paper 1: Comprehension and Practical Criticism

Many teachers are apprehensive about exposing their students to the risk of 'unseen' Comprehension and Practical Criticism examination papers.

- Are you one of them?
- Why?

Think again about the Aims and Objectives of the syllabus.

- If your course has been planned to achieve these aims, and to give students wide experience of reading, of reflecting about what they read, and of expressing their responses to it, why won't they be equipped to cope with the Comprehension and Practical Criticism paper?

Paper 2: Set Books

Remember that this is an 'open book' examination. Students have access to their text when they write Paper 2. This means that questions can be closely focused on specific parts of a text, as well as requiring knowledge of the whole. The emphasis is on the ability to produce a detailed critical response, which draws closely on the evidence in the actual text.

- Does this explanation of the nature and function of the Set Books examination affect your choice of text?
- Does it affect the way you plan to teach those texts?

Students are allowed to annotate the texts which they bring into the examination.

- Does this affect your choice of texts?
- How will it affect your teaching of them?
- In what ways might your approaches to coursework texts, and to set books, be developed in order to enable students to acquire and practise strategies which will stand them in good stead in the terminal examinations?

Paper 3: Coursework

Decisions about coursework texts need to be made in conjunction with those made about set books if the course is to be coherent. Links between texts tend to be most easily made, and are most easily seen by students to be made, in terms of content and theme. But if it is the only way chosen of making connections, this may create difficulties at times in directing students away from content and ideas towards considerations of form and style. The fact that the set books are arranged partly by genre might help to extend your criteria for choice beyond the list suggested above.

The 'rules' governing your choice are simple. Among your six named coursework texts, you must include:

- a second Shakespeare play
- a work of non-fiction
- poetry.

Since you cannot rely on every text, and every task set on it, being equally successful for every student, it is advisable to name and work on slightly more than six texts. (For a further discussion of these separate elements of the coursework folder, see below.)

Course Planning: internal and external deadlines

As well as making your choice of texts, you need to plan how to use the available time. Although seen as a two-year course, A level actually has at best only five terms at its disposal. Since AEB 660 places a much heavier reading demand on students than most traditional courses (a minimum of ten texts, not including those on which the student chooses to base the Extended Essay), it is necessary to plan the use of time very carefully.

The final deadline for submitting samples of coursework for moderation to the Moderator is 30 April in the final year of the course. In the run up to that it is necessary to consider various facts of A level life, the details of which will be peculiar to each centre, and to anticipate the need to fix internal deadlines.

1 Introductory period

- Will you or won't you include one?
- Can you spare the time? If not, why not?

Bearing in mind that only six weeks before students become A level students they are GCSE students, it seems hard to expect them to make the leap into A level study without at least offering them some stepping stones. These do not have to be constructed out of great slabs of content or literary history; they can equally well be composed of introductions to ways of working, approaches to texts and kinds of writing which the students will be using throughout the course.

- How much of your first term do you feel able to devote to an introductory period?
- Which texts will you use?
- How will you use them?
- Will you expect any outcomes for the coursework folder?

2 GCSE resits

These are not so much of a hazard as O level resits used to be – or are they?

- How many of your group are resitting subjects?
- What effect will this have on your teaching programme?
- What do you plan to do about this?

3 The Extended Essay

This will take a great deal longer than you think to set up and to complete, especially the first time. It is essential to start the process early (i.e. during the Summer term of the first year of the course at the latest), so that students can do the necessary reading and drafting during the Summer holiday.

- What sort of arrangements will you make for individual supervision of Extended Essays?
- What deadlines will you set for the production of drafts and finished product?

4 'Mock examinations'

- When do you have yours?
- How much time do they take out of your teaching programme?
- What do you plan to do about this?

5 Internal assessment and standardisation

As mentioned above, you need to submit your sample folders to your Moderator by 30 April in the final year of the course.

- When will you set the deadline for the completion of folders?
- When will you carry out internal assessment?

Alongside sorting out the planning framework for your course, taking these internal and external 'givens' into account, you need to decide the content for each term. As with so much of the work with AEB 660, this is for you to decide in terms of your own teaching situation. The syllabus Aims and Objectives indicate the kind of curriculum and learning experiences you should try to provide, and you should look on the coursework folder as the opportunity for the student to deploy and demonstrate evidence of a range and variety of reading, and a balanced variety of ways of writing about that reading. 'Imaginative' as well as critical responses are encouraged in this syllabus, as they are in GCSE, always provided that they are clearly rooted in the text which has been studied. In addition, there is the opportunity in the folder for a student to include examples of his or her own original writing, not necessarily connected directly to a text. In relation to all the decisions made about AEB 660 coursework, whether it is choosing texts for study or setting assignments on those texts, the crucial questions for teachers are:

- Why am I choosing/doing this?
- In what ways does this text/this piece of work earn its place in an A level Literature coursework folder?

3
THE NATURE OF
ASSESSMENT
—

This book is concerned with coursework and its assessment, but of course the coursework, as has already been suggested, is best undertaken as an integral and interlinked part of the whole course and not as a separately taught 50% of the course. The following statements about the Assessment Pattern from the AEB's syllabus contextualise the coursework in terms of the marks available for the whole course:

Assessment Pattern

Paper 1 *Written paper, Comprehension and Practical Criticism*
2 hours and 30 minutes (including 15 minutes
recommended reading) *(22% of the total marks)*

One question from each of Sections A and B:

Section A Comprehension and practical criticism of a poem or poems.
A choice of questions will be offered.

Section B Comprehension and practical criticism of a prose or drama
passage or comparison of two passages. A choice of questions
will be offered.

Paper 2 *Prescribed Texts*
3 hours and 15 minutes (including 15 minutes recommended
reading time) *(28% of the total marks)*

One question from each of Sections A, B, C and D (Shakespeare, Poetry, Plays and Novels).

There will be two questions on each text framed so that they are capable of being answered in 45 minutes.

Candidates will have access to their set texts in the examination, enabling them to provide a critical response in some depth with close reference to the texts. The texts may contain the students' own notes (in any blank space or page, but the use of other materials such as critical works, dictionaries and additional notes is not allowed.

Coursework *(50% of the total marks)*

Eight units: it is anticipated that most essays will be between 800 and 1200 words but work outside these parameters will not be penalised on length alone. *(8 × 15 marks)*

One extended essay of about 3000 words. *(60 marks)*

In addition to the 'Notes for Guidance', the AEB also produces 'Notes for Guidance on Criteria for Assessment of Coursework Folders' for 660, which are designed to help standardise the assessment of work. Both the 'Notes for Guidance' and the 'Notes for Guidance on Criteria for Assessment of Coursework Folders' are regularly updated in the light of current practice. Like all such descriptors, they need to be used in conjunction with actual material to be made operational, and this is one of the tasks which will be undertaken during the course of this book. It is essential, though, that these criteria (or the equivalent band descriptors in whatever coursework syllabus is being followed) are both very familiar and thoroughly internalised before assessment is undertaken.

Band 1 (0–4 for Coursework; 0–17 for Extended Essay)

Work may contain the rudiments of ideas, though response is likely to remain at a basic narrative level. Better work will be comprehensible even where there is evidence of poor and inaccurate expression.

Band 2 (5 for Coursework; 18–23 for Extended Essay)

Writing within this range will show some acquaintance with the text, with some attempt made to move beyond basic narrative treatment. Work *may* show a modest degree of engagement with the ideas of a text, as well as some knowledge and understanding, although treatment will require more substance and organisation. Topics may be handled implicitly rather than explicitly at this level.

Band 3 (6 for Coursework; 24–29 for Extended Essay)

Work in this category will show a fair grasp of texts at a narrative level and some willingness to handle ideas. Textual references may be incomplete; more relating of texts to topics may be needed, but writing should provide evidence of some success in reading and reflection, expressed in a basic framework of argument. Candidates may provide evidence of greater engagements with texts, even though treatment will still require more substance, better organisation and presentation.

Band 4 (7–8 for Coursework; 30–35 for Extended Essay)

Candidates in this range will show that they know the text, and have attempted to present a view. Understanding and some degree of interpretation will be evident; expression will be clear, even where it could be more carefully organised and better focused. Some emerging competence may be revealed in linking texts to topics, and in composing a coherent framework of argument.

Band 5 (9 for Coursework; 36–41 for Extended Essay)

Writing in this range will reveal careful, well-engaged work, characterised by good textual awareness and a willingness to handle related ideas. Work will be soundly organised and substantial, and go beyond a mere recitation of received ideas on the content of a text. While engagement with the texts may lack individual critical edge, candidates at this level will show skill in relating a text to a topic, and reveal that they are capable of developing and maintaining an argument.

Band 6 (10–11 for Coursework; 42–47 for Extended Essay)

Candidates will provide evidence of accomplished, well-written work, which covers the chosen ground with thoroughness and skill. Work may contain some of the qualities to be found in the highest mark range. Even where the critical engagement and handling of ideas may not be entirely assured, there will be clear evidence of comprehensive textual understanding, discrimination and capacity for argument. Some critical flair may be apparent.

Band 7 (12–15 for Coursework; 48+ for Extended Essay)

Work at this level will show coherent, fluent organisation of material and of argument: accurate textual awareness and sharp insights will be revealed. The writing will often be exploratory, thorough and succinct. The candidate will be skilful in making free use of texts to achieve effective connections of ideas and themes. An individual 'voice,' confident, sensitive and thoughtful, will be evident. There is likely to be a considerable range of achievement here, from very good to outstanding. Full marks may be given where appropriate.

These descriptors have been developed out of descriptions of student work. They are not meant to be absolute and prescriptive statements to be checked mechanically against the work, but are attempts to make general statements which have proved to be true for many pieces which have been closely examined.

In assessment, we are trying to find evidence of particular skills which we take to be the following. Candidates are learning to choose appropriate ways of:

- identifying
- selecting
- ordering
- discriminating
- contextualising
- presenting
- illustrating
- constructing
- developing
- sustaining
- hypothesising
- analysing.

The descriptors need also to be applied within the particular context of the wording of the task and the conditions under which the piece has been produced. It is important that assessment should be done by the teacher who knows what these conditions were. There is a large difference between the achievement of a candidate producing work after very little class discussion of a text and the task, and the work of another student who has experienced a great deal of close attention in class to the particular approaches and structures which can be adopted for the production of an essay. In the same way, those students who can find a structure and approach of their own are showing additional skills to those who have had a structure given to them. Some teachers are often worried about the extent to which drafting and redrafting are 'allowed', and the extent to which teacher support may be given. This is not quite as straightforward as the request for a 'rule' might imply. What one is trying to do in assessment is to evaluate what the candidate can do. Clearly, credit cannot be given to a candidate for the work which the teacher has done; instead the focus must be on the contribution which the student has made. Nevertheless, there may well be circumstances in which detailed teacher guidance will allow a student to achieve much more. In such a case, the teacher is assessing what the candidate has been able to do. It may be that one candidate receiving a lot of help can do no more than literally incorporate the teacher's suggestions; this does not suggest that the candidate has shown additional skills even though the final piece may be an improvement over the first version. Another candidate, however, may be able to make considerable use of the advice given and may be able to transform the original work. Clearly, the second candidate deserves more credit than the first. It is absolutely vital, therefore, that some indication is given on the cover sheet of each essay of the amount of class discussion, teaching time, preparation time and teacher support which has been given. This will enable subsequent readers of the piece to contextualise the marks given and to be able to understand the process of assessment. Similarly, it is most useful when teachers are making their assessments that they should make reference to the skills achieved in their comments on the piece. In this way, Moderators and other subsequent readers will be able to share in the process of assessment.

The issue in assessment, therefore, is not what 'rules' have been adhered to and broken, but what skills the student has shown. This is also applicable when we consider pieces of work which are other than the 'standard literary critical essay'. We all think that we know how to assess a piece of this kind (although we often use an auto-pilot approach which can lead to difficulties), but there is frequently anxiety about assessing other kinds of work. Some questions to be asked, if the student has adopted a different kind of form, are:

- How effective is this choice of form?
- What skills are being shown?
- How well does the piece communicate its intentions?
- What response is there to subject matter, ideas, themes, form, style?
- Is the piece effectively structured?
- Can the student develop ideas and perceptions?
- Is there a personal critical voice?

The task itself, however, is vital, and wording needs to be considered very carefully. In A level assessment we are not looking for skills in isolation; we are looking to see how well, how fully, how deeply, how perceptively the task has been undertaken. Thus there is a crucial interplay between the student's own response and skills and the task itself. Difficulties come when the student may have responded to the text but not to the precise task set. We shall be encountering some examples of such cases later in the book. It is particularly important, however, that during their coursework, students develop their skills of responding centrally and directly to the set task, for this is a skill which they will need in the other 50% of the whole assessment, the examinations.

For us, the fundamental aspects of assessment are these:

- that it engages as fully as possible with what has been done
- that it results in comments which help the candidate to develop
- that comments reflect the reader's experience of the work
- that it is for the benefit of the student
- that it is carried out in a teaching context

- that it is carried out in the context of the conditions under which the work has been produced
- that it arrives at an appropriate mark.

All this goes to suggest that the process of assessment should be an open one, where the teacher keeps formative as well as summative purposes in mind. If this is the case, then it is important that the candidates are themselves as familiar with the band descriptors as the teachers. Much effective work has been done in the classroom on all the materials which the Board provides: the Aims and Objectives; 'Notes for Guidance'; the band descriptors. Many centres have also found it invaluable to supplement a sharing of these with a sharing of previous years' Examiners' Reports. Several teachers have reported that students can become adept at assessing their own work as well as that of their peers and that they learn a great deal about how to go about their own work by undertaking these tasks.

One final point needs to be made about assessment. Different centres adopt very different procedures regarding the assessment of students' work during the course. Some give no marks at all; others give marks and grade-descriptor comments to every piece; some rely in the first instance on self-evaluation and peer-evaluation. Whatever method is adopted, it is important that there is a final stage of assessment at the end of the course when the teachers produce final marks for each piece of work individually as well as for the completed folders as a whole. When more than one teacher is involved in the teaching, it is also vital that a professionally organised internal moderation procedure is invoked, so that the centre can be certain that all of its marks and the centre's final rank order is indeed fair. With large centres this is a time-consuming and difficult job, especially at a time of year when it has to be done for almost every course which the department offers.

Despite recent proposals, it is expected that teacher assessment or coursework will continue to have some part to play in examinations and in the assessment of the National Curriculum Key Stages. Institutions should recognise the additional workload which this imposes on teachers during the end of the Spring and the first half of the Summer terms, and plan accordingly to provide them with proper conditions in which to do this work professionally. Rather than seeing the 'examination period' simply as the weeks during which external examinations take place, institutions should also include in it the earliest coursework deadlines and dates for the submission of marks to Moderators, as well as practical examinations and orals. Adequate time needs to be provided, since there are no short cuts to effective internal moderation. Those centres just beginning coursework as part of their A level, or those planning to do so, should make sure that those in charge of their institution understand fully that properly planned periods of time need to be given to moderation once the folders are completed. If this stage of the work is done satisfactorily there should be no major problems at later stages.

Once internal moderation has been completed, a sample of work will be sent to the Moderator, according to whatever instructions are received from the Board. The Moderator may make adjustments, but his or her work will also be sampled by the Chief Moderator who again may make some adjustments. All this work will have been undertaken on aggregated marks, and the point of using marks is to spread the candidates in appropriate rank order throughout the mark range. Only at the final stage of the proceedings – the Award which takes place in July at the Board's office – do grades become a consideration. At that stage (and not before), the awarders will tie grade boundaries to specific marks. It can, therefore, be very misleading to candidates to inform them of grades even on the coursework component before the final results are published. Neither teachers nor Moderators have access to the information about grade boundaries before the final Award stage.

4

SHAKESPEARE

—

- Is studying a coursework text different from studying a set book? Should it be?

- Is teaching a Shakespeare play for coursework different from teaching it as a set book? Should it be?

The fact that students of AEB 660 must study two plays by Shakespeare should force us to confront the question, 'What are we doing this for?' head on. Following on from Key Stage 4 of the National Curriculum, one answer would obviously be, 'Because we're told to.' In the statutory Programmes of Study for English at Key Stages 3 and 4 we have the interesting phenomenon of an otherwise free choice of reading material, with one author only named and prescribed for study at the higher level, and that author is Shakespeare. Teachers are likely to explain the reasons for this according to their own background, training and particular leaning towards one or more of the schools of English teaching described by Professor Cox in the English Working Group's report, *English for Ages 5–16* (June 1989). All of these positions give teachers a basis for selecting texts and methodologies through which to study Shakespeare, and will no doubt have guided their selection of other coursework texts and their overall planning of their A level course to some degree. However, behind this prescription lie a number of assumptions about the nature and status of classic texts which are very relevant to teachers and students of literature, and which A level students could usefully be encouraged to start exploring through their compulsory study of two Shakespeare plays.

On the most basic level, the Shakespeare coursework text can be chosen for all sorts of reasons: to complement the set text, or to contrast with it, to contribute to a theme running through other parts of the course, or to stand more or less on its own. There is an embargo on choosing any play from the Set Books list, but centres sometimes limit their choice still further by failing to look beyond the tragedies and comedies. There seems to be some strange, covert, but well understood consensus that certain plays are 'A level plays' or 'GCSE plays' and teachers would do well to consider this when making their choices. For example, *Macbeth*, *Romeo and Juliet* and *Twelfth Night* are becoming fairly staple fare at GCSE. Is it really advisable, therefore, to revisit them at A level? If the decision is made that it is, then the questions which must be asked are:

● What will A level work on this play look like?
● How can I help students to move beyond the understandings which they reached on their first encounter with it?

Choices of Shakespeare texts are also often guided by what is currently in production nationally. As a recognition that these are plays, not poems or novels, this is to be welcomed. The syllabus suggests that, 'a review of a theatrical performance . . . in which the production is related to the text, will be acceptable as one unit'. Teachers intending to take up this suggestion should heed the warning that, 'the review should consider how far the production satisfactorily realises what is in the text, and in what ways it illuminates the text beyond the potentialities of the printed word alone.' Reviews of live performance are an obvious possible outcome from coursework, but if they are to be successful for the full range of candidates they need very thorough and careful preparation, which involves more than simply reading the text in advance. Many A level students are inexperienced theatre-goers, and lack the context within which to position a director's interpretation of the play or an actor's performance. Terry Gifford has written interestingly about his work on encouraging response to live performance in *English in Education* (Spring 1987; Vol 21, No 1), and offers much good advice on preparatory and follow-up work surrounding a visit to the theatre.

On the other hand, the availability of versions of Shakespeare on film, often used simply as a more accessible version of the written text lower down the school, invites close textual study, in which detailed comparisons can be made at a level beyond superficial details of presentation. A class might work in small groups to generate a number of comparative studies of aspects of Polanski's and Nunn's *Macbeth*s, and seeing Olivier's and Branagh's film versions of *Henry V*, in conjunction with a consideration of their historical contexts and dates of production, could open up discussion of alternative readings which could then be applied to further texts. After studying *Othello*, viewing Nunn's production, with particular emphasis on the presentations of Desdemona and Emilia, could challenge conventional interpretations of both these characters, and prompt a revisiting of dominant readings in other texts.

So, what are we doing it for? Is it just because Shakespeare is part of our national heritage, that 'knowing' his plays is part of being 'educated' and more of him must be better? Or is it also because of the opportunities which these plays offer for understanding more about handling plot, character, themes, symbols, language, the possibilities of plural readings, how drama works and about the roles of the reader/ director/actor/audience?

Given that the ultimate aim in studying any text should be to arrive at as full an understanding as the student can achieve at the time, and to be able to articulate that understanding, then studying a text for coursework or for a set book examination isn't that different. What is different is the kind of work students can do on the way to achieving that understanding. On the Set Books paper, the questions focus on the single play, possibly on a single section of that play, and require a complex combination of close knowledge of the text, and the ability to revisit it freshly from an angle not necessarily prepared for or of the student's own choice. The coursework text can provide opportunities for developing the necessary skills and the essential understanding of the genre, but at the same time students can be encouraged to be more independent in the aspects of the text they select for thorough study.

Whatever the task, however, it is beneficial to students to devise tasks which allow them to show an understanding of the play as a whole. The task which follows does that and also allows students to show how they can conceptualise their response in different ways. The design is illustrated by a particular moment in the text and the candidate is also able to show her understanding of characterisation, mood and themes by concentrating on that particular moment. It is important, however, that the student is able to show knowledge of the particular context of the given task (in this case stagecraft and design) as well as to show knowledge of the text itself.

EXAMPLE 1

Task

(a) Invent a design concept for your production.
(b) Choose a short moment from the text, and apply your concept to the design.
(c) Write character instructions for the actors playing the selected moment.

(a) Invent a design concept for your production.

In the last scene of *The Winter's Tale* Leontes admits

> I am ashamed: does not the stone rebuke me
> For being more stone than it?

Using Leontes's own words, I decided that the Sicilia scenes should be entirely in stone, giving a very bare, cold image. I set Sicilia in Florence in the late fifteenth century, shown by the Florentine arcade around the back of the stage, and a central (life-size) statue of a madonna. However, this statue is more than an indication of time and setting; it is the force of good in the play and it is this statue which will come to life in the last scene when Hermione returns to the play. In the first acts, however, the stone around the Madonna is crumbling (heading for ruin – as Leontes is in the first scenes) which symbolises the decay of the court scenes and how the forces of evil are destroying Leontes's world.

Sicilia, Acts I, II, III. The set is very bleak and bare.

The costumes for the first acts are the Italian Renaissance fashions of the time (see pictures) in maroons, dark greens and browns (fairly dull colours contrasted later with brighter costumes in Bohemia). However, Hermione is dressed slightly differently. She is dressed in the red or maroon colour with a blue cloak (or black) that paintings of the madonna were so often depicted wearing at that time; this symbolises her purity and goodness. Leontes is dressed in black, symbolising the evil forces surrounding him in the first three Acts.

Costumes: Sicilia

Madonna adoring the Christ Child (detail) by Perugino (1450–1523). Hermione's costume should be based on this.

Italian Renaissance fashions c.1480–1510.

Bohemia is set in the Italian countryside and the set itself shows the growth and new hope Perdita and Florizel bring as the crumbling arches are covered with flowers. The madonna is still present, symbolising that forces of good will always remain somewhere, despite temporary disappearance.

Bohemia. The set is predominantly green – symbolising the growth after the decay and ruin.

The costumes in Bohemia are fairly colourful and are set in about the 1540s. The women are wearing fairly long simple dresses, decorated with flowers. Perdita is wearing a white dress which symbolises her purity and contrasts with the black Leontes was wearing earlier. She, too, is wearing flowers in her hair to decorate the costume. The men's costumes are fairly plain. However, Autolycus (like Hermione) is wearing a slightly different costume. His is more intricate and the base colour is the same red or maroon that Hermione was wearing, symbolising his unwitting aid to the forces of good in the play. An example of what his costume might look like is given below.

Costumes: Bohemia

(a)   (b)

(a) *A farm-lad. I thought this costume would be good for the Clown.*

(b) *A shepherd. This would be the basic male costume for Bohemia.*

Autolycus: his costume is a little more intricate.

I felt in my production that it was important to show the passage of time clearly to the audience. When we return to Sicilia the costumes are becoming much more recognisably Tudor. (A change in style in the 1550s which took place throughout Europe.) They are all more intricate, except for Leontes who has exchanged his black costume for a religious dark brown plain costume, symbolising his reformation and loyalty to the madonna (Hermione). Hermione, in her madonna costume, has changed places with the statue and in the last scene she comes to life. It is at this moment, back in the drab Sicilia court, that the family are reunited and the magic of *The Winter's Tale* is really felt.

(b) Choose a short moment from the text and apply your design concept to its design.

For this section I have chosen Act II, scene I (lines 59–99) where Leontes accuses Hermione for the first time. Leontes is evil or possessed with evil spirits which will threaten the existence of the good forces found in Hermione. His black costume (symbolising evil) reflects his part as he cruelly accuses the confused Hermione of her 'crime'. The set itself is very dark, symbolising how Leontes is in darkness (he does not see clearly) apart from the madonna which is lit up showing the ever present forces of good and how this scene depicts the initial battle between the two. Hermione's true goodness is shown as she sits, breathless (it must be remembered she is pregnant – another link with the madonna) after playing with Mamillius. It is obvious to the audience (as it has been from the start of the play) that she is innocent; her costume and her manner portray this fact. In Leontes's speech lines 81–84, the lords which have been surrounding him and almost supporting him see there is no possibility that Leontes is right and move away from him slowly until they are standing between the arches. This is symbolic of the decay; the set is crumbling and heading for ruin and so is Leontes. He has lost whatever strength and beauty he once had which is shown in the set. It is almost as if the lines of W. B. Yeats's poem 'The Second Coming' fit this world:

> Things fall apart; the centre cannot hold.

The scene is very physical as Leontes's anger shows itself; his frustration as his world crumbles around him, a fate which can only be described as self-inflicted.

(c) Write character instructions for the actors playing the selected moment.

Leontes

In this scene I want to show the evil side of the madness which has temporarily overcome Leontes. I feel that in this crucial scene where Leontes first accuses Hermione, there must be no compassion. In this scene the power of evil will temporarily overcome good and the actor must be prepared to look and sound cruel; his manner must be both verbally and physically threatening towards the pregnant Hermione.

At the beginning of the moment Leontes is standing on the right of the stage with his lords around him and Hermione is sitting on the left of the stage. Leontes's first lines are spiteful and insulting and should be spoken that way:

> for 'tis Polixenes
> Has made thee swell thus.

Leontes use of 'thee' here was intended as an insult a very degrading tone of voice should be adopted. After her rather indignant reply Leontes turns to the lords for support with the words:

> You, my lords,
> Look on her, mark her well.

Throughout his speech lines 64–78 here should be a lengthy and tortuos build up. The atmosphere is very tense and it is Leontes who creates this. He must move towards and around the sitting Hermione; he is threatening her.

On his final line 'She's an adultress!' Leontes should almost lunge towards Hermione and then pull back. Hermione has stood up and backed away from him (towards the statue). Leontes must take almost a sadistic pleasure (while angry) in her response and is moving around the stage showing his high nerves. The lords have begun to move away from Leontes, having fully realised the error of his accusations. He persists in his attack on Hermione:

> You have mistook, my lady,
> Polixenes for Leontes.

He then rather sarcastically adds the lines:

> O thou thing –
> Which I'll not call a creature of thy place.

At line 87 Leontes looks round at the lords and sees they have moved away. He calms down and attempts to put his case more clearly to them, appealing to them for support:

> I have said
> She's an adultress; I have said with whom:

However, he looses his calmness by his anger at the words 'bed swerver'. Hermione's response to this speech ends my selected moment. What I was attempting to convey was my feeling that here, and at the point where he rejects the baby, Leontes is at his most cruel. There must be no indication here that Leontes will repent; in the scene the audience must feel no sympathy for Leontes plight. As an audience, we support the good forces, and it is Hermione who is the personification of these forces.

Hermione
It is perhaps because Hermione is the personification of good that some productions can fail to breathe life into her part. It must be remembered that Hermione is being accused for the first time of crimes which are so obviously false. At first she even thinks Leontes is joking:

> What is this? Sport?

After he has insulted her she takes his temper more seriously and although Hermione is strong she must show a little fear. This fear would help to add dimensions to her character; she is human and she feels threatened by Leontes' aggressive behaviour:

> How e'er you lean to th' nay-ward

However, as the tension builds up she is more and more afraid. As Leontes shouts the words 'She's an adultress!' she stands as he lunges towards her and she backs towards the statue, as if she is seeking protection. After a pause it is almost as if the statue has given her strength. She ventures the words:

> Should a villain say so.

She appeals to Leontes from the protection of the madonna:

> you, my lord,
> Do but mistake.

Throughout Leontes's speech (lines 82–94) Hermione is gaining strength; she senses that Leontes is losing support and it is here she almost becomes a madonna; the babe she will bear will bring new hope to the world. She now replies to his accusations strongly, moving back towards Leontes, arguing with strength.

> No, by my life,
> Privy to none of this. How will this grieve you,
> When you shall come to clearer knowledge.

Here she forsees the future. Her presence has become almost goddess-like; her vision is remarkable and is her strength against such adversity.

I want to show in this scene that just as Leontes is overpowered by evil forces, Hermione is supported by good. Her initial fear will breathe life into the part and her transformation is almost as sudden as that of Leontes. It has now become a battle between good and evil forces and in *The Winter's Tale* the forces of good, inevitably, will triumph in the end, with the reunion of the family in the last scene.

This candidate arrives at a workable design and thereby shows familiarity with stage design and how stages can be used. She has economically shown how the design can work for different parts of the play and has a clear sense of where the audience is located in this open staging. The ambivalence of the several images – particularly of the crumbling Madonna which serves both as an image of Leontes (the crumbling) and also of Hermione (the Madonna) – shows this candidate's theatrical sense and also her keen awareness of the ambivalence of the text. It is particularly notable that Bohemia is set in an earlier time period than Sicilia and it would have been interesting had the student expanded on any problems which this might have given her in regard to the earlier scenes of the play. The red shows awareness of thematic development in the play. The student's lack of differentiation between magic and religion suggests an interesting and provocative angle on the nature of the reconciliation scene. Some of the complexity of Leontes's state of mind in the early scene is caught in the instructions to the performers. As the original teacher noted about this piece:

> Why Renaissance Italy? The Madonna idea? The time-shift might be more obvious – but the arcade imagery with the statue is a touch of brilliance. You've carefully thought out a governing idea and pursued it logically and thoroughly. It comes from the text, and illuminates it in turn. The style and mood of the period – Machiavelli and Botticelli together – suits the text very well.

While it might have been encouraging to see the candidate exploring the multi-valenced nature of the text by means of a more detailed analysis of the choices she had made, this is work worthy of an A grade and in AEB 660 terms merits a mark of 12.

It is sometimes useful, however, particularly in a mixed-ability group, to present tasks where students can respond at their own level. The following very broad topic was designed for these circumstances, and designed also to allow the teacher to see the extent to which the development of the main character had been understood from the teaching so far.

EXAMPLE 2

Task

Chart the changes in Lear's character and his state of mind throughout the play.

In the beginning of the play we see King Lear as a very dominating King who likes to get his own way. He is bad tempered and sometimes loses control of himself. Lear confuses his parental functions with his regal functions; he expects his daughters to flatter him like his courtiers. In Act I we see Lear as an old man who has decided to abdicate in favour of his daughters. In return the daughters have to pledge their loyalty by declaring their love for Lear. Goneril and Regan pledge their love to Lear and they are given a part of his kingdom. Lear is satisfied. He turns to his favourite daughter Cordelia, expecting her to declare her love. Cordelia replies

> Unhappy that I am, I cannot heave,
> My heart into my mouth. I love your majesty
> According to my bond, no more nor less.

Lear is outraged at this and he loses his temper. He decides to disclaim Cordelia and banishes her from his kingdom. Although Lear is angry there is perhaps some sense of disbelief and saddness at the outcome. Lear decides now to divide his time between Goneril and Regan.

After Act I, there is some change in Lear, his authority is starting to crumble, and he feels betrayed by Cordelia, his favorite daughter. Her turns to his bad daughters Goneril and Regan and tried to seek shelter at Gonerils instead she turns against Lear. Goneril shows her true character and the brutal way she treats Lear, she tells him of his disorderly knights and instead of wanting a hundred she says she only wants fifty. This makes Lear react with a violent hatred manner, and reduces him to tears.

Lear feels humiliated, and he starts to realise what a stupid fool he has been in believing that Goneril loved him. he sees what a grave mistake he had made in banishing Cordelia because he knows that she was the only truthful one out of her sisters. he feels intense rage towards Goneril for her treatment against him and how deceitful and greedy she had been. At the same time Lear feels a lot of grief and saddness for Cordelia, and he is regretting the mistake he made. Lear at this point feels totally rejected and hurt.

At this stage of the play Lear is losing his grasp on sanity and this scene has contributed to his insanity he is suffering for the consequences that have been brought upon him.

Lear then decides to go to his other daughter Regan. Lear starts to wonder if Goneril's cruelty is beginning to affect his mind. Lear's suffering is worsened when he finds Kent in the stocks and cannot believe that Regan and Goneril did that to Kent, Lear is overcome by emotion. He is confronted by Regan and Goneril. At this stage Regan also shows her true character and she also turns against Lear. They argue against Lear saying that he should reduce his retinue and she also turns against Lear. They argue against Lear saying that he should reduce his retinue or disperse it completely. Lear is now virtually at breaking point, he tries to be patient but it is not in his nature

The connection between Lear and his daughters is now severed. he sees their brutality and ruthlessness to try and get rid of him. A storm breaks out and this signals the collapse of Lears state of mind.

The change in Lear is seen in the way he speaks reflects the change in his mind. Lear is less fiery and is almost subdued, but although his mind is imbalanced he starts to see his faults and what he has done wrong.

While in the storm Lear identifies it with his cruel daughters and feels his wits are beginning to turn.

In Act III, it reveals the change in Lear and that he has turned mad, this is seen in the world being turned upside down reflects the disorder in Lear, he is confused, this is also due to the suffering Lear has had to go through and the brutal treatment by his daughters, and his grief and sadness for Cordelia. Lear's state of maddness is revealed when he stages the trial of Regan and Goneril, this shows the justice that he wants. Lear now feels that the suffering that he has gone through has changed him into a different man, it is as though he is not the man who rejected Cordelia, but now he feels flattered to be answered 'ay' and 'no' to everything he said.

In Act IV shows Cordelia's return, she is ready for forgive Lear. Lear is taken to the French camp near Dover where Cordelia waits. It seems that Lear recovery to almost sanity is due to music, although his maddness has gone, he is more quiet and tranquil not like the Lear that was seen in Act I. He is very confused he seems to think that he is in hell and he says that he is senile, it is revealed in this Act. Lear and Cordelia meet for the first time since

she was banished and it reveals the mutual affection between them, this is
after the battle that is lost. Lear and Cordelia are taken prisoners by Edmund,
but now it semms that Lear especially is happy and at peace with everything,
his feelings are much more open.

sadly Cordelia is murdered, but Lear does not believe that Cordelia is
dead, soon after this Lear dies of grief.

Throughout the play we have seen Lear change, in the beginning we see
him as a very domineering person, through his suffering we see him turn
insane, but in the end although Lear dies in anguish, he is at peace inside his
body.

This candidate is able to detect some changes and to pinpoint a few of the
important moments in the text. She makes some sensible general points
about the scenes she discusses, although she is never in as complete
control of her material as one might like. For example, at the end of the
first paragraph she quotes from Cordelia rather than from Lear and thus
blurs the focus of her commentary. She finds it difficult to substantiate
her points by detailed reference to the text and there are times when she
becomes very vague: 'At this stage of the play . . .', for example. While
the student is aware that the changes in Lear can be seen from the way he
speaks, she is not able to go further to illustrate or analyse. As is
frequently the case when the writer is not confident in conceptualising
the material, most of the writing is about the early scenes of the play and
there is therefore very little space left to 'chart' the changes. Even when
responding on the most basic level – when retelling the story – the
student sometimes becomes confused about the sequence of events. As
her confidence wanes, so her syntax also becomes less secure. There is no
clear sense that the student did in fact begin with a 'chart' and she is
unable to define and pinpoint the specific changes in Lear with sufficient
clarity to illuminate. While there is some potential in this piece, perhaps
to be shown later when the skills of illustration and analysis are learned
and put into practice more confidently, this piece is not yet of A level
standard and merits an N grade with a mark of 5.

5

POETRY

—

In the past, Paper 1 of AEB 660 included questions on a set poetry anthology, as well as Practical Criticism on 'unseen' poetry. The anthology was not there as another set book to be studied in its entirety, but rather to act as a springboard and stimulus to the reading of a wide variety of poetry during the course. The idea was admirable, but the attempt to assess this range of reading in an end-of-course examination was doomed to failure, scuppered partly by students' and teachers' fear of wide open questions which invited students to choose their own material on which to base their answers, and partly by their consequent efforts to cut the whole thing down to size by prepackaging the reading and the possible answers into 'poems about death' or 'Ted Hughes as a nature poet'!

The requirement to demonstrate that a substantial amount of poetry has been read during the course has now been split between the unseen poetry question on Paper 1, and the compulsory unit on poetry in the coursework folder, which the syllabus refers to as, 'the poetry of one or more writers or poetry exploring chosen themes'.

When choosing the material on which this compulsory unit will be based, teachers need to think carefully about the reason for its inclusion in the coursework folder, and about the place of poetry in the course as a whole. They are not necessarily one and the same thing. While it often seems to be taken for granted that the study of poetry is the finest manifestation of the study of literature, it is also something which students tend to find most difficult, and about which many feel least confident. In setting the 'unseen' questions, the examiners are free to choose from the whole range of English poetry, from any period and any author. Centres should therefore be aware of the dangers of concentrating too heavily on twentieth century writers, at the expense of extending their students' experience of poetic style, form and technique. The habit of using single poems as practice runs for the Paper 1 questions is also problematic, unless students have developed some sense of context for their reading. These warnings seem to argue for the planned introduction throughout the course of a considerable amount of poetry from different periods and in different styles.

An effectively designed poetry assignment allows centres and candidates to focus some of their work on poetry very specifically and can enable students to demonstrate their critical skills in interesting and personal ways. It is also one of the main areas of the coursework where students can learn and practise reading skills which they can profitably transfer to the end-of-course examination. It can offer opportunities for individual research, presentations, seminar-type sessions and collaborative work which can contribute to the production of a range of coursework assignments, individually suited to students. If the single compulsory unit in a folder is judged on superficial criteria, such as the number of poems discussed, it may appear to be far less than the sum of its contributory parts. It needs to be seen as part of the larger context of the student's wide-ranging reading of poetry, and framed in such a way as to demonstrate the student's effectiveness as a reader and writer. Some possible ways of doing this, apart from the study of a single author, or critical writing about poems connected by subject matter or theme, are to:

- work on a number of anthologies and their introductions, with a view to understanding the personal nature of anthologising. This could lead to students making personal anthologies for specified purposes and audiences. The assignment would include the students' own introductions to their selections, explaining the reasons for the choices which have been made.
- work on a number of poems within specified parameters. The assignment could invite students to select a limited number of poems from those read, which would illustrate the variety and range to be found within, for example, a particular period, culture or genre.

Students should be allowed to include in their folders the best piece of work they have done on poetry during the course (and they should have done many). One centre, offering an integrated course where students were seen as writers as well as critics, used the poetry assignment to focus on the work of one poet, in this case Seamus Heaney. Many different approaches to the poetry were introduced in class and students became alert to the various ways in which readers read and writers write. It was encouraging, when moderating the whole centre's work, to see how many candidates had been stretched by this assignment.

The first candidate chose to write her own poem after her study of Heaney. She was thus challenged in two ways – as a writer and as a critic. The assessment problem was to ensure that what was being evaluated in this piece was not in fact the student's own poetry but her critical response to poetry – both her own and Heaney's.

EXAMPLE 3

Task

This student decided to write a poem about one of her own early memories after studying Heaney's poetry and then to draft and redraft her own poem.

A study of Seamus Heaney's work and my own

1st Draft

Waiting by the shore
The horizon housing many of the scattered-fractured islands,
I stood solitary of my own accord
This – almost my second home,
Was my world of complete enjoyment.
A place of extremes.

The sea gulls screached
Almost in harmony with the crashing ocean,
Enjoying the freedom of this mythical orange evening.
The salty scent of the filtered air
Filled my lungs to their full capacity
Breathing with the rhythm of the swelling sea.

My creation stood proudly by my feet
The great fortress of sand resisting the perpetual tumbling of
    the briny waters.
It's military flags standing defiantly on top of the
    battlements
Each carefully shaped by my own delicate hand.

The enemy was approaching – it's front-line was firing hard,
Stones were tumbling fiercely along with the travelling sand.
I watched as the tall walls crumbled,
And my fantasy destroyed.

Maybe tomorrow I could rebuild this barricade to the sea,
With the sea wind circling it's water front
And drawbridge outlined by shells.

2nd Draft

Waiting by the shore
With pictures of scattered islands on the far off horizon,
I stood solitary and on guard.
This – almost my second home
Was my world of complete enjoyment
A place of all extremes.

The sea gulls screeched
Almost in harmony with the crashing ocean,
Enjoying the freedom of this mythical orange evening
Salty scents of the filtered air
Filled my lungs to their internal limits
With the rythmn of the swelling sea.

My creation stood proudly by my feet,
The great fortress of sand resisting the perpetual tumbling of
    the briny waters.
It's military flags stood defiantly on top of each battlement
Each carefully shaped by my own delicate hand.

The enemy was approaching – it's front-line was firing hard,
Stones were tumbling fiercely along with the travelling sand.
I watched as the tall walls crumbled,
And my fantasy destroyed.

Maybe tomorrow I could rebuild this barricade to the sea
With the sea weed circling it's waterfront
And drawbridge outlined by the shells.

3rd Draft

THE CASTLE

Waiting by the shore
With scattered islands glowing on the far off horizon,
I stood solitary and on guard.
This was my second home,
My world of complete enjoyment
A place of peace and tranquillity battered only by the sea.

The gulls screeched, almost in harmony with the crashing ocean,
Enjoying the splendour of the mythical orange evening.
Salty scents from the filtered air
Filled my lungs to their internal limits
Expanding with the rhythm of the swelling sea.

My creation stood proudly by my feet,

The great fortress of sand resisting the perpetual tumbling of
    the briny waters.
Its military flags stood defiantly on top of battlements
Each carefully moulded by my own delicate hand.

The enemy was approaching, its front line was firing hard
Stones were tumbling fiercely along with the solute sand.
I watched as the tall walls crumbled
And my fantasy destroyed.

Maybe tomorrow I could rebuild this barricade to the sea,
With the sea weed circling its water front
And reinforced walls of stone.
They'd laught at me, I know,
For my dreams, thoughts, and games
But nothing would stop me from building
My dreams and fantasy creations.

4th Draft

DREAM CASTLES

Waiting by the shore
With scattered islands glowing on the far off horizon
I stood solitary and on guard.
This was my mind's second and secret home
My world of complete enjoyment
A place battered only by the sea.

The gulls screeched in unison with the crashing ocean
Enjoying the splendour of the mythical orange evening.
Salty scents from the filtered air
Filled my lungs to their internal limits
Expanding rhythmically with the swelling of the sea.

My creation stood proudly by my feet,
The great fortress of sand resisting the perpetual tumbling of
    the briny waters.
Its military flags stood defiantly on top of battlements
Each carefully moulded by my own delicate hand.

The enemy was approaching, its front line was firing hard
Stones tumbled fiercely as the beach was made to move.
I watched helpless as the tall walls crumbled
And my fantasy destroyed.

Maybe tomorrow I could rebuild this barricade to the sea
With seaweed circling its water front
And reinforced walls of stone.

They'd laught at me, I know, scuttling here and there,
But the only thing to stop me would be
The intrusion of that same crashing ocean.

A thorough look at how Heaney writes of his own childhood

Observations
- Heaney's writing is just full of descriptions – all of which producing strong visual pictures for the reader to see.
- Heaney writes of his own childhood with emphasis on both major and minor events, but every occasion is written about with great detail showing characteristics of a good memory.
- He does not write his poetry in a uniform style, for example the number of lines in each stanza differs and the number of stanzas in each poem also vary.
- Heaney has a tremendous way of describing things he sees into literary pictures. A poem he writes about 'Blackberry-Picking' shows us this very well. The words he uses portray the scene so effectively that the reader almost finds himself experiencing Heaney's own feelings. He describes everything in great depth incorporating visual impressions, tastes, textures and smells, all of which emphasising the vividness of the images.
- Heaney uses many onamateapaec words throughout his poems on childhood. Examples of such words are 'gargled', 'plop', 'slap', 'squelch'. These words help me to associate the poetry with incidences in a childhood, as they seem to refer to descriptions a child would give. Heaney seems to adapt his poetry back to childhood by using these words adding an essence of innocence.
- In some of Heaney's childhood poems one gets the impression that he is somewhat uninvolved with the subject matter. It is only when he nears the end of the poem that we see any real emotion or personal involvement with the poem. It is here that the reader can acknowledge the importance of the poem for Heaney. An example of this is a poem called 'Digging' when Heaney leaves emphasis on the last stanza, showing the reader his real meaning to the poem,

> Between my finger and my thumb
> The squat pen rests
> I'll dig with it.

- There are also poems where Heaney looks back at his childhood with more emphasis on his own feelings. For example 'The Follower' shows how Heaney's feelings for his father have changed.
- Most of the poetry has a mixture of maturity and childhood innocence. Heaney writes poetry about his childhood in such a way that the reader gets a balance of both innocence and grown up, adult feelings.

Study of my own writing (with Heaney's)

Reading my own piece of writing after studying Heaney's, it seems extremely unfinished. Heaney's poetry seems to read so smoothly and easily without the additional necessity of rhyme that I feel I need to alter a few lines.

I feel that the subject I've chosen to write about is fairly minor event yet is something that I can easily remember and know I did many times. In the same way Heaney writes about such things as 'Blackberry-Picking' which he must have experienced many times yet manages to write successfully about.

I think it's very hard to write poetry about popular subjects like the sea without producing cliches. It would be very easy to be influenced by other poets descriptions and not to discover ones own interpretations and original ideas. I think Heaney also does this, by describing with such depth and originality we can define one of his great poetry characteristics.

Modifications to my own work

- I've made several modifications to my piece of work which I made in light of observations made about Heaney's. The biggest difference from all three drafts to the forth one is the ending. I found that the poem seemed almost incomplete without the addition of some reflective thoughts. This is something that I feel Heaney does a lot of in his poetry.
- Other modifications are simple changes in phrasing and words. I tried to replace words that did not really bear any great strength to the subject matter with others of more power. I tried also to show both feelings/ thoughts and descriptions of what was happening.

What have I learnt?

- I think that it is very easy to be influenced by one author if one concentrates solely on his work.
- I found the drafting process very interesting. Although my modifications were not very major I found it very helpful to experiment with different arrangements of words to see which were best fitting.
- Studying Heaney's work definately helped me in producing a piece of writing (although mine is a long long way from his standard!) It was interesting to see how he combined both innocence and maturity in his writing and helpful when trying to do the same.
- Heaney's strong emphasis on description is something that influenced me a great deal. Description in poetry to me is everything and Heaney seems to use reactions from all the senses to add emphasis. This I found extremely helpful when writing.

This candidate decided not to use the formal critical essay framework for her piece but to offer a series of reflections. While many of the opening comments about Heaney's work are very general – they could all do with some expansion and analysis – there is some grasp of the structure of poems and the shifting tone and perspective, particularly in the sixth observation. There is some awareness of problems associated with writing in the student's observations about her own work. Several significant features of the style come under scrutiny in the student's redrafting, although it would have been worthwhile had she written at some length about these. There is some awareness of shape and form and some attention to themes and subject matter in this piece. The student is aware of several features of content and style and is beginning to appreciate the interrelationship between them. Overall this piece merits the award of a D grade and 8 marks.

EXAMPLE 4

A second example of a poetry assignment comes from the same centre and concerns one poem, 'North'.

Heaney's poems were initially discussed and read in class. The draft manuscripts of 'North' were also looked at and then the candidate developed these first impressions. He drafted a first copy and then over a period of three weeks revised and corrected it. The final piece was submitted three weeks after the task suggestions were handed out to the class.

Task

Examine Heaney's manuscript version of 'North' and discuss, in detail, the way in which the poet has refined the poem. Analyse the use of language and comment on any changes that have been made in the process of writing.

The process of writing poetry is a long and complex one. 'North' only goes to highlight how the composition of a poem is not just a case of spontaneous brainstorm, but can be a long, methodical process of constant revision and sometimes drastic changes. I propose to study the progressive refinement of 'North' in an attempt to understand why the changes were instigated and whether they serve this intention, or only cloud it further.

The opening scene of North sets a very distinct mood, not only expressed by the word meanings, but also through the short, sharp sounds of words such as 'thunder', 'hammering' and 'shod'. On studying the earlier versions we can see that this word use was intentional since Heaney has gone to great lengths to omit the soft drawn out words, such as 'curved', from the final poem. The two distinct impressions I get from the poem, was one of power, that of the 'thundering Atlantic', but also the lack of excitement which one would have expected. The word 'secular' having a double meaning: firstly something that slowly, but persistently, goes on forever, and secondly something not profound, unmagical. Both meanings are applicable in this instance, and reflect the mood of this verse. He proceeds to describe Greenland and Iceland as 'unmagical' and 'pathetic', words which leave little to doubt on how he feels about them.

The use of 'suddenly' at this point, brings about a complete turn in the poem, and is all the more effective when it was moved immediately next to the previous description. The word is the pivot to a complete change of language and mood, as well as Heaney's change of heart at what faces him. The full magic of the Atlantic is revealed to him, and he begins to conjure up pictures of the 'fabulous raiders', the Vikings, conquering the great ocean lying before him.

The central part of the poem is devoted to descriptions of the Vikings, describing their culture, it overflows with admiration. The first revision of this section was the way the Vikings were portrayed as 'fabulous raiders', whereas in a previous version they were called 'beautiful adventurers'. The reasons for the change are relatively clear. The word 'beautiful' evokes an image of a hero in tights wielding a dagger, reflecting little of the rogueish nature of the Vikings, whereas 'fabulous' indicates admiration on behalf of the poet, but at the same time captures something of the warrior charm possessed by these men.

The admiration Heaney seems to show is reflected in his description of the burial procedures of dead noblemen. The lines:

> measured against
> their long swords rusting

seems to be a picture of the Viking dead lying with their swords lain across their chest. Heaney then recounts how he saw the warriors lying in 'the solid bellies of stone ships', inferring the traditional burials of Noblemen in burning seacraft. These lines remain unchanged throughout Heaney's revision, indicating that he was very sure of how it would be interpreted. The section of the dead warriors finishes with their 'ocean-deafened' voices warning me, lifted again in violence and epiphany'. Is he suggesting by the 'lifted again' that through his poetry he can recreate the same violence and glory?

'Thor's Hammer' is obviously the symbol of the great might of the Vikings, and how they controlled the 'geography and trade' of the Atlantic. Yet the basis to their lifestyles is that of 'thick-witted couplings', 'revenges' and 'hatreds'. In the original scripts he adds terror, but unlike the pettiness of revenge, terror indicates a calm, collected kind of evil, quite out of character. Therefore it is altered to the words 'behind-backs', insinuating the back-stabbing, gossiping society.

At this point the original version ends with the line 'poets incubating the spilled blood'. But obviously Heaney felt this was inadequate to express all that is contained within the poem, although I feel it goes some way to explaining Heaney's motivation in writing the poem. I read this as if he felt that the poet could recreate and bring back to life the glory of the Vikings, including the violence and 'spilled blood'.

The final section of the poem is about the poet's mind, his ideas, thoughts and how he creates a poem. He describes the brain as a 'word-hoard' an area to 'burrow' into the 'furrowed brain'. The repetition of the sound 'urrowed' adds both rhythm and a sense of digging deep for ideas. This explains Heaney's original phrase: 'worm of your thought'.

The final two verses are written in the style of advice to fellow poets. The first of the two uses the concept that ideas are like lights, and Heaney says of this:

> Compose in darkness
> Expect aurora borealis
> In the long foray
> but no cascade of light.

It is interesting that this imagery is used at this late stage yet preparation to give this effect seems to have been considered even up to the first two lines. For Heaney leaves out the line 'hammered under light' not only to make it appear dull, but also to create the feeling that there is darkness, and the picture of the Vikings were the aurora borealis in the poet's mind.

The second of the verses is just a final word that the poet must 'trust the feel of what nubbed treasures' their 'hands have known.'

To conclude Heaney's changes seem in the most part to be for the sake of clarity and to improve imagery. I did feel however that in places the poem lacked rhythm, but for the most part had a fluency which accompanied the desired mood, for example the pace soon quickens when Heaney begins to imagine the Vikings coming across the sea. I found this kind of studying most informative and helpful in seeing how a poem is constructed. Heaney's feverish revision only goes to prove that: 'What is written without effort is in general read without pleasure.' – Samuel Johnson (1709–1784)

The candidate has used his manuscript sources well and this has alerted him to several significant features of Heaney's redrafting process. He is attentive to the effects of words and to the effects achieved by structure and form. He makes several effective and thoughtful deductions about Heaney's processes and intentions on the basis of the various versions. The candidate has clearly appreciated the poem and has enjoyed teasing out meanings and implications. The piece itself is carefully and consciously structured and shows confident critical skills of B grade work, meriting a mark of 11.

It should be noted that these students were offered a wide range of possible topics for their coursework essay on Heaney and were also able to negotiate their own task and title with their teacher if they preferred. In this way, not only were all the students able to write about something which particularly interested them, but they were also able to stretch themselves and to show their personal responses partly by means of their individual choices.

EXAMPLE 5

A very different kind of task also arose from an extensive study of poetry. This particular task has as its context a study of themes in different historical periods.

Task

Discuss the use of the natural world in expressing spirituality, comparing the different relationships between the physical and the spiritual and the consequent impact in 'Regeneration', 'Dover Beach' and 'The Banished Gods'.

'Regeneration', 'Dover Beach' and 'The Banished Gods' involve the natural environment in three seemingly different but interlinked ways. I aim to look at these differences and similarities in order to achieve a deeper understanding of the poems and their impact on me. I will first discuss how I think the poet has used the natural world in the poem after which I will look at the effect of articulating an expression of spirituality in such a manner. I will then attempt to draw some conclusions about the use of the natural world in the poems and the consequent effects.

Contrasting pace and speed of development throughout the poems appears to be a useful indication of contrasting uses of the natural world. In 'Regeneration' by Henry Vaughan, the narrator is taken from a 'rocky pinacle' through a 'faire, fresh field', to a 'banke of flowers'. The rapid movement from location to location is used to reflect a quickly developing spirituality. The picture of nature is used both metaphorically and as an initial context for the spiritual awakening described. The youth begins his walk in the high-spring yet 'was it frost within,/And surely winds/Blasted my infant buds, and sinne/Like Clouds eclips'd my mind'. From this point onwards, his path becomes 'rough-cast with Rocks' and now the cinematic sweep through nature is reflecting his own spiritual development. His repose in a 'faire, fresh field' and then his entrance into a grove marks part of his change; perhaps the intellectual acceptance of a Christian Saviour. It has occurred with no Divine intervention save for the call into the field and could be seen as an initial understanding found within himself. 'The aire was all in spice/And every bush/A garland wore; Thus fed my Eyes,' and so he can now perceive a beauteous garden as the 'sunne shot vitall gold.' This satisfying picture of nature is used to express an initial awakening and it is a 'rushing wind' that eventually gives him some use for the Eares and led him to asking the Lord to make him re-born or 'dye before my death!' The wind works as an original and powerful image for the rushing realisation of conversion but it is reinforced by the use of the Biblical symbol of the Holy Spirit. The natural world has been used by Vaughan both as a real setting in a specific time, as a metaphor for the narrator's spiritual state and as a basis for the symbols representing the Divine intervention leading to conversion.

In Arnold's 'Dover Beach,' although the use of the physical world is in a description of a static scene it has a similar two-fold purpose as in 'Regeneration.' The pleasing picture of a calm sea at night, the French coast, the English cliffs and tranquil bay lit by the moon as recounted by the narrator purveying the scene, is given a sad edge in the last two lines of the final stanza describing the movement of pebbles: 'With tremulous cadence slow, and bring/The eternal note of sadness in'. This is the spring-board for the narrator to apply the scene before him to what sees as the spiritual state of the earth. By comparing the full tide and 'the Sea of Faith' we are told how now all he hears is the 'melancholy, long, withdrawing roar'. Rather than letting the real picture become a metaphorical sight as in Regeneration, the real setting is kept in the background as Arnold uses it as the image for the narrator's simile. The effect is to preserve the sharp reality of the situation which is imperative for the final stanza when the narrator pleads with his love to remain true in order to displace the disillusionment he feels with the real world. It also makes the last image more striking. Although it is a symbol for a world that has lost its direction and has replaced spiritual aspirations with earthly struggles, it combines with the narrator's physical situation. 'The darkling plains' on which the ignorant armies clash can be both the godless plains the earth has become and the scene which stretches before them that night. Arnold uses the physical description to make the poem's setting very clear as well as to convey a spiritual state.

This mixture of the metaphorical and the actual is also employed by Mahon in 'The Banished Gods' but with a different emphasis. Three silent, static and people-less scenes are described with an economy of words that makes them chillingly simple and their purpose clear. The 'seas sigh to themselves/ Reliving the days before the days of sail' and the silent moor 'shelters the hawk and hears/In dreams the forlorn cries of lost species', representing a landscape that mourns the time when man had not disrupted nature by culling the penguins and whales and killing whole species. These anthropomorphisms are snap-shots showing how man has rejected the natural world in favour of his cars, chemicals and computers. In this way, the natural world is more central to the poem than in the previous two, for it is not only used to reflect spirituality but also to make a statement in itself. The rejection of nature re-echoes the rejection of spiritual existence represented by the gods banished to the stone, water and trees of the seething moor. The banished gods seem to me to highlight nature being transcended and spirituality connected with the creation and the reverence for the roots of man being renounced. The use of the natural world is complicated by its ambiguous function as a central theme in itself as an expression of spirituality. I see the scenes as a clear and poetical method of encapsulating the lost natural world. They are isolated areas far from man's trade-routes or boundaries that remain irrevocably affected by his empty living. They are representational of the physical nature of the earth, in turn echoing its spiritual nature.

The use of the physical world in expressing spirituality can be seen to have several purposes. To begin with, it gives the discussion of a spiritual state a physical context. In 'Regeneration' and 'Dover Beach' it provides a present time and a real initial situation. In 'Regeneration' the connection to God's creation is also striking and very appropriate in a narration of a Christian conversion. The connection with a time, place and central character makes the description of spirituality relevant as we can apply it to real characters. In the 'Banished Gods' it makes not just a connection to one person and place but to the whole world. However, the rejection of nature is not just a connection to the physical world in this instance but also the centre of the poem lamenting the loss of spirituality and ties to our origins.

A more fundamental intention in using the natural world is to make the expression of the internal state more tangible to the reader so that he can visualize it. The connections already established go a long way in doing this, but the use of the natural world as a metaphor also does this. This is most noticeable in the intensely personal experience of 'Regeneration'. To have simply retold the emotions and development he encounters during his conversion would not have communicated nearly so well as a journey through a landscape reflecting his state of mind. It also gives weight as a poem, suggesting it has some poetical value that makes it worth an interpretative account. All these factors go to make the poem a lot more vivid and original.

A strand running through the use of the natural world in this poetry is the knowledge that it is a universal language. Everyone can recognise the picture of rejected nature in 'Banished Gods,' the relevance of the sea-scape in 'Dover Beach' and the physical world of 'Regeneration.' This visualisation and identification with the poem's central image must be the first step in finding the poem's core or inner reality. However, if they are really using a universal language, would readers with no religious background be able to understand the experience and exploration? 'Banished Gods' presents us with the least problems since the natural world takes centre stage and no specific religious figure is implicated. Mourning for the loss of 'soul' can be identified with regardless of religious ideology. 'Dover Beach' creates a back-drop that sets up the character as sympathetic. His lament for a lost spirituality and even more significantly the need for love in a desolate world is once again understood despite religious standpoint. It is 'Regeneration' that causes the most difficulty. In relating a Christian conversion, the poet must be aware of the difficulty in communicating this to people with no personal experience of this kind. I believe Vaughan has done everything within his literary powers to express his experiences so that even if the concept cannot be grasped, the development can be followed and visualised and his emotions conveyed. This discussion concerned with communicating a spiritual state with the reader has inevitably centred on the poem's theme and the part played by the natural world has seemed to be largely incidental. It does prove, however, to be an easily identifiable setting providing many familiar images that enable a reader to 'gain access' to a poem. In this way, the natural world does prove to be a 'universal language' when discussion of a spiritual state may not be.

The impact of all three poems is very strong indeed. The sharp picture of reality they all painted was a way into the investigation of spirituality. The clear expression of the internal state was done by comparing the physical world with the spiritual as in 'Regeneration's' external spring and internal frost, by creating a vivid real situation and by reflecting the spiritual state of a character or the world using the environment. The connection made with the mental context of the reader by all three poems ensured communication on some level. I found the poems dramatic, poignant and clear in their objectives.

This is very confident work which clearly fulfils the criteria for the award of an A grade. The writer immediately established his argument and illustrates perceptively, with depth of appreciation and succinctness. He is fully aware of the ways in which these poets use the outer world as mirrors of their inner world. He discriminates perceptively between these three very different poems and draws thoughtful and illuminating generalisations out of his study. His central thesis is to the fore throughout (although it perhaps gets a little less interesting in the repetition of the final two paragraphs). He is able to extend his criticism of the poems to more general reflections and to show the reader something of his own interests and preferences. His own style is elegant and persuasive as well as full of his own response. This is distinguished work high in the A grade and merits an AEB 660 mark of 14.

The original marker had drawn the student's attention to what she felt to be a relatively weak final paragraph, where the writing had failed to do full justice to the impact which the three poems had had on her. Partly to encourage further dialogue between teacher and student, the centre has a section of the cover sheet called 'Student Comment (Post-Mark)' where this student had been able to reflect on the teacher's comment and wrote:

> The restricted nature of the final paragraph was mainly due to the word limit that bound me to keep it clipped. I agree that it did not do justice to the impact the poems had on me, but it was meant to be a brief conclusion to an essay which I had hoped had expressed this.

6

EXTENDED ESSAY

It has sometimes been the case that teachers have decided either to adopt the Cambridge coursework syllabus or AEB 660, or to reject it, because of the Extended Essay requirement (see Bill Greenwell, *Alternatives at English A Level*, *passim* and p. 62). But many teachers have also found that while the Extended Essay appears to be an insuperable hurdle to students before they begin work on it, by the time they have finished it a dramatic development in their maturity and in the quality of their work is discernible.

However, just as teachers working on AEB 660 for the first time may find it hard to keep the balance between coursework and work for the examination in proportion, so they may also find it difficult not to let the Extended Essay take over too much of students' time and attention. It certainly is an important part of the whole course, and offers students opportunities for choice and independent study which they may not get from texts read by the whole group. It also provides opportunities to learn to sustain an argument and conduct a comparative study of aspects of several texts, all of which is good preparation for the kind of work some of them will be expected to do in higher education. All the same, it needs to be kept in perspective and the whole process to be managed properly if the Extended Essay is going to be as successful as possible.

In the interests of keeping it in proportion, it is worth remembering that while the Extended Essay is worth four of the short coursework essays in terms of marks, it is only expected to be about 3,000 words long. To discuss several texts in any detail, this is not a particularly high expectation of length. Expressed in percentage terms, the Extended Essay is worth 17%. Although this is the largest single amount awarded, it is still less than any of the other component parts of the examination: eight coursework essays (33%), two Paper 1 questions (22%), four Paper 2 questions (28%). In itself, it will not compensate for failure to produce the three compulsory units of coursework, or for a well-balanced complete folder.

Managing the Extended Essay effectively requires forward planning. Decisions have to be made about the amount of time which can be devoted to it, and the quantity and nature of teacher assistance that will be useful and necessary. We suggested in Chapter 1 that the work should be spread over the Summer term of the first year of the course and the Autumn term of the second, to allow students sufficient time for the necessary reading and drafting. Whenever you position it in your course, you will need to allow time for introductory discussion, for decisions about possible texts, and for notifying your Moderator in good time of the topics and texts chosen by the students.

In the experience of many teachers of AEB 660, it is the close links and co-operation between centres and Moderators which have contributed to the success of this part of the syllabus. The requirement to submit students' titles for their Extended Essays before they begin to write has several effects. The first is that teachers spend a lot of time with students as a group and individually, working with them on defining their chosen area of study and helping them to form their topic into a workable title. It is customary for three (or in some circumstances, two) texts to be studied, and students are encouraged to read widely when they are thinking about a possible topic. The Moderator can advise centres about possible pitfalls in the topics – especially over the suitability of chosen texts and the wording of titles – or raise questions about the point of undertaking a particular study. The Moderator can also help teachers to engage in continuing supervision of their students while the essay is being written. The following pages show titles which were submitted to one of us by students, who also included notes on what they were aiming to do in their Extended Essays. The Moderator's comments, shown here, were then used by the teacher as a basis for further discussion with each student. This example may be helpful in indicating ways in which the beginnings of Extended Essays can be developed into something more focused and productive, hopefully without taking ownership away from their writers.

1 Does literature's rebel ever succeed? *(1984, Brave New World, A Clockwork Orange)*

Or should it be 'Do rebels ever succeed in literature?'? (I quite liked the original title!) Looks as if the candidate has a clear idea of what he wants to argue, which is good. Ought to be careful not to introduce too many references which can't be developed.

Rather than spending time distinguishing between rebellion and revolution, which could get very complex and possibly take it off track, I feel time might be better spent characterising the nature of the individual rebellions as presented by the authors.

At first I thought it was a pity all the protagonists were male, but on reflection I think they are an interesting bunch. The section of the essay dealing with society and their relation to it ought not to be 'generalised' but rooted in the texts.

2 To what extent does childhood affect adulthood? *(David Copperfield, Oliver Twist, The Go-Between)*

What's here is drawing on a very narrow range of examples – perhaps the focus is *too* tight, and the answer too apparently obvious.

Don't yet get any sense that the candidate is going to distinguish between the texts, or their authors. Wouldn't it be an idea to work 'backwards' and look at the ways each writer uses/writes about childhood experience?

3 A consideration of Greene's novels as thrillers *(Brighton Rock, The Power and the Glory, The Heart of the Matter)*

'Thriller' embraces a huge variety of different texts by different authors – can it be used unproblematically, on the assumption we all know what sort of thriller we are thinking about?

Which is the title – this, or 'Greeneland . . .'? They aren't really quite the same, and there's a good essay in either. Lots of material here, but it needs direction. Don't lose the bit about morals.

4 A study of the power of the dystopia *(1984, Brave New World, Island)*

Plenty of close reading here – risk of getting submerged in detail unless candidate can find a point of view to illustrate or an argument to pursue. There's a lot in the notes about control of society, but perhaps these questions might also help her find a purchase on the material:

Why do we construct/read dystopias? To frighten ourselves? To warn? To reflect on the present? When did Huxley and Orwell write? Are their novels relevant/irrelevant now? What are the effects of their books on readers today?

5 Can the detective story be considered as a serious literary genre?

I still have hopes of this one! The original booklist looked interesting but references have shrunk to *Moonstone*, Conan Doyle and A. Christie. Feel the candidate is right to look at how detective stories can handle contemporary issues – feminist detective writers are interested in issues of social control etc. of particular concern to women, e.g. Sara Paretsky's woman detective and health care scandals, etc. Unfortunately, A. Christie does very little of it!

Is the question 'Is the detective novel a literary genre?', in which case the answer is obviously 'Yes'. Or is the essay aiming to make some value judgements about popular fiction and 'good' literature, and when the detective story becomes the latter? (I'm just asking – the candidate seems to have a line she wants to argue, which is fine – I'd just like the fight to be a fair one, which the original list of texts, with the inclusion of *Edwin Drood*, Rendell, and Highsmith as well as Collins, suggested it might be.)

6 The corrupting influences of money/material possessions *(Bleak House, The Great Gatsby)*

This will just end up as two accounts of what happens to the main characters, unless the essay is extended to look more broadly at the effects of money on the lives of the characters, and to think about what the writers are saying to us about the power of money.

She could start by making some lists of who has money – and what they do with it – and what sort of people they are. This will reveal that the power of money is a lot more complicated than she's suggesting in her outline at present. She ought to look at the endings of her novels as well as the middles.

7 Thorns in the side of Utopia *(The Handmaid's Tale, 1984, A Clockwork Orange)*

Apart from the quibble that they aren't, of course, Utopias, this looks like quite a clear and simple account of the main characters' roles in these novels. Perhaps she should try to look at why the novelists need these characters – what their actual function is, what they make us think about, and what their effect is on us as we read.

8 'Man's love is of man's life a thing apart, 'tis woman's whole existence.'

Candidate has collected a vast range of references – there's too much here. How about focusing on men, or women, in her chosen texts – she seems to want to write about their attitudes to love and sex, and the constraints society places on them. I think a concentration on George Eliot's women – or Eliot's and Lawrence's female characters, if she wants to do something comparative – would be a lot more effective and manageable. I'd choose George Eliot's women myself – they are such a rich and varied range, and I have the feeling the candidate finds them interesting too. There'd be more than enough to write about if she used *Middlemarch* (Dorothea + Celia + Rosamund + Mary Garth) and *Mill on the Floss* (Maggie + Lucy + Mrs T + the aunts), for example.

Arriving at a title which is a good hook to hang an Extended Essay on is not an easy matter. Some centres require students to write a brief statement of intent, outlining the texts they propose to read and what they intend to do with them; others make use of whole-group sessions at which students present their plans and refine them as a result of questions from their peers; most rely on individual tutorials with students to work out a title and a structure for the essay. Some departments involve colleagues not actually teaching A level at the time, who have areas of expertise from which students can benefit. Whatever methods are used to develop the Extended Essay topic and monitor its progress, the aim must be to enable each student to produce his or her own well-argued piece of independent work.

In helping students to formulate titles, teachers need to beware of:

* proposals which link together several texts which have little apart from superficial features in common, unless the student can demonstrate that he or she has more than a superficial commentary in mind
* grandiose wordings which might conceal mere plot summaries and character sketches, for instance, 'an examination of . . .', 'representations of women in . . .', 'a study of . . .'
* proposals which mix genres, such as fiction and autobiography, without acknowledging that they are doing so
* titles which may take students no further than 'giving an account' or 'describing' their texts.

Given the kind of support suggested above, students ought to be able to arrive at a final title for their essay to which they will work very closely. The discussions which they have with their teachers at an early stage are crucial in helping students to grasp whether or not they are responding directly to the task they have set themselves. This skill will also have clear relevance to their examination performance later on, and is often a lesson usefully learned first through the Extended Essay.

Once the material has been chosen, the skills necessary to produce a sound Extended Essay are not essentially different from those needed for success in other aspects of the course. Students need practice in reading for an identified purpose, making accessible notes, contextualising their comments in a brief, economical way, selecting illustrative material appropriately, developing an argument and pursuing it. The Extended Essay adds the extra demands of ranging across several texts, handling a substantial amount of material and sustaining an argument at some length. The qualities which distinguish a successful essay from the less successful are the sense of direction and purpose which the essay conveys, and the drive with which the argument is sustained. As far as methods are concerned, an essay where the writer is working within a conceptualised framework which supports the overall argument, and is moving freely between texts to demonstrate relevant points, will be much more effective than one that remains at the level of the content of texts, and moves from one to another in a sequential way. Some drafting and redrafting is bound to be necessary. Teachers frequently find that to begin with the first draft is far too long and repetitive. Working with students on this can be useful in helping them to see that it is better to illustrate a range of points once rather than demonstrating the same point over and over again.

Whatever strategies the centre adopts for monitoring the progress of the Extended Essay, it is important that students feel that they are being supervised and have regular meetings, however brief, with the teacher responsible, to ensure that the work is progressing at an appropriate pace. Many students enjoy the personal nature of the study and want to go on and on refining and redrafting their essay because it is the part of the course which is most obviously their own. Deadlines are crucial, and need to be set within the planned framework of the whole course. They will have to be set for the following stages:

- decisions about topic
- decisions about title
- first draft to teacher
- final product to teacher.

The other work of the course must continue, and teachers also need to be aware of any other coursework demands being made on their students in other subjects, and the deadlines for these.

As far as assessment is concerned, the essay is also the area of the folder that can sometimes be overvalued by the teacher, particularly among weaker students. The reasons are easy to see: students have put a lot into their work; they have often responded more enthusiastically to this than to anything else; they have clearly developed; they have become involved in the course. It is sometimes difficult to remain objective about the quality of the final product when one knows how much work has gone into a project, and there is often considerable bunching of marks in the high D to low B range which, in the experience of Moderators, ought really to be in the low N to low B range. The examples we have chosen to include, therefore, are concerned with the difficult area in the N/E range which teachers are, on the whole, reluctant to award.

EXAMPLE 6

Task

Examine how Harold Pinter provides us with the poetic reality of life in three of his plays, The Caretaker, A Slight Ache *and* The Dwarfs.

In this essay I intend to do three things, examine the setting, and how the audience is aware of the importance of the setting and the insecurity of the characters in the three plays I have studied and see how this relates to the stage setting. I also intend to examine how the characters relate to each other. For example, the relevance of characters talking to each other, and neither listening. A common occurrence in Pinter's plays.

I intend to do this by looking at all three plays, examining them carefully and then comparing them with each other. The first play, *The Caretaker* is about basically a tramp who goes to live with two brothers, and it is mostly about his point and views on life, and the conflict between the three of them. *A Slight Ache* is a short play about a husband and wife who have a big garden in which an old man stands at the gate on the road selling matches, although he never seems to sell any. The couple invite him in but can get nothing out of him. *The Dwarfs* is another short play about three men who seem to have separate rooms in a building. This is mainly about one character who believes he sees little dwarfs. This like many of Pinter's plays is also based mostly on conflict.

Firstly I shall study the stage setting in all three plays, the audience awareness of this and its significance.

In all of Pinter's plays, whether it be any of the three I am studying, or *The Birthday Party*, *The Dumb Waiter*, *The Hot House*, and many others, he keeps the stage setting very simple and precise, and often without any scene changes. For example, a vase on a table in the corner could be of immence importance at some stage of the play.

In *The Caretaker* for instance, as in all plays, there is a description of the stage setting at the very beginning. This has a very detailed description of how the stage should be set. 'A room. A window in the back wall, the bottom half covered by a sack . . . boxes containing nuts, screws etc. . . . a lawn mower, or shopping trolley . . . a bucket hangs down from the ceiling.' This is just a few points which Pinter makes to ensure that the stage setting is exactly how Pinter saw it when he wrote the play. In the play, the bucket, which catches the drips from the ceilings plays an important part, if only in order to start a conversation off and to show a little of each character. For example at the beginning of *The Caretaker* Davies says 'I told him what to do with his bucket. Didn't I? Look here, I said, I'm an old man . . .' so enabling Pinter to explain Davies' character and let the audience know a little more about him. This is not the case all the time, but is one of the reaons that Pinter is so precise about how the stage should look. Almost everyone of the Props on the stage is used. Each one has its own significant purpose.

In another of his plays, *A Slight Ache*, there is a difference. This play is one of the few contrasts to the others. In this play, the description of the scene is quite brief, and there is also a scene change during the play. As it says in the description 'both indicated with a minimum of scenery and props'. In this case, Pinter chose to leave the rooms bare in order of making sure the audience concentrates on the characters, specifically the matchseller and not surrounding objects. This again shows us how Pinter uses scenery and props to a great extent. Since there are only three characters in the whole of the play, everything must be concentrated on them and since the characters personalities are more or less self-explanatory, there is no need to use props to help with anything.

Looking at the third and final play, *The Dwarfs*, this is a sort of median, although there are not a great deal of props, there is more than there is in *A Slight Ache*. The Scene changes quite frequently and finally a short scene in a hospital when Len is taken ill. However although the number of props is less, they are still used in the same way. For example, the cups, saucer and sugar etc. tells the audience the two people Len and Pete are having tea, and Len is playing a recorder. This allows the play to start naturally and comfortably, and consequently lead into the main story line.

Therefore we can see that the stage setting, scenery and props, is very important for several reasons. First of all, the props are used to introduce characters, allow them to explain their personalities and attributes, and give the audience a general idea of what they are like. On the other hand, a lack of props and scenery makes sure the audience concentrate on the characters and what they are doing. Finally, props are often used as a conversation starter and the beginning of a scene. Consequently, I have shown how props, scenery and scene changes contributes to audience awareness of what is happening and why, and therefore allows a clearer picture of what the general play is about.

Having established Harold Pinters use of stage setting, i.e. props and scenery etc., I now intend to look at how the insecurity of his characters relates to this. In all of Pinters plays, there is always one, and often more than one, character who is insecure in some way or another.

A prime example out of the three plays I am studying is Len out of *The Dwarfs*. Although all three of the characters, Len, Pete and Mark appear to be insecure in some way, at certain areas of the play Len is definitely the most, especially towards the end. At the start of the play, Len is playing the recorder, something not a great deal of grown men do. This immediately gives us some idea of Lens character. An interesting point in this play is when Len asks Pete what he is doing with his hand. Pete is in fact doing nothing with his hand except for resting it palm upwards but Len persists on asking what he is doing with it. The way the statement is used, (Len was previously talking about his job) once again gives us an idea of Lens slight madness and insecurity. I feel that he is suddenly upset or annoyed about talking about his job and although he does take a true interest in Pete's hand, it is also a way of changing the conversation. 'I've got the makings of a number one porter. What are you doing with your hand?' Obviously a human hand is not exactly a prop but it shows how Pinter uses such things to show a little of a persons character. Another point, and probably the most effective is when Len is sitting in his room on his own. This part is really the first real sign of Len's madness as he is sitting on his own, talking to himself 'There is my table, That is a table. There is my chair . . . That is a bowl of fruit . . . This is my room . . .' It is quite clear to see that Pinter has used the props, and only the props in order of showing Lens madness.

The Dwarfs isn't the only play where this happens, it also occurs in both the others I am studying and many others. For example, *The Caretaker* shows this in some areas. One of the areas of this is again at the beginning of the play. This is where Davies (the main character in the play) is talking about his shoes. He talks for a long time, telling the listener a tale of how he got them from the monastery. From Pinters use of the shoes, leading to the tale, we learn that Davies was apparently previously a tramp, we learn some of the places he's been to, and generally a little about his past. There are many other examples in *The Caretaker*, all showing Pinters use of Props to help show the insecurity of characters, such as the electrolux under Astons bed.

Finally *A Slight Ache*. To start with, there is the Matchseller with his tray and his matches. These are obviously the most important props in the play, considering that the story is about a Matchseller, and consequently his matches. That fact that he never sells any of his matches, shows us that the old Matchseller is not completely normal, insisting on standing outside the garden gate everyday, in wind or rain or shine. The man in the house eventually gets fed up with him and asks him inside in order of finding out something about him. The matchseller making no use of the chairs until he is more or less forced to sit down, once again shows us that he is not completely sane.

We have seen that Pinter uses props a great deal in order of showing the audience what the characters are like, their values and their bad points. He also uses props to show how one character relates to another and consequently on showing the insecurity of one character, he can show the difference with others.

Having written about the above, I now intend to talk about how the characters relate to each other, in Pinters plays, whether it be through language, imagry and so on.

I shall start with *The Caretaker*, probably one of the best examples with the three characters, the two brothers Mick and Aston, and Davies the caretaker. The way Pinter shows how the characters relate to each other is by the conflict between them. In *The Caretaker*, the characters are all in conflict against each other. Often what happens is there are two characters complaining about another character. An example of this is Act 3. Mick and Davies are alone in the room, and throughout the beginning of the Act, up until Aston walks in, the two of them are complaining about him, mostly Davies moaning with Mick agreeing. He complains about how Aston never talks to him, he doesn't give him a knife to cut his bread, he complains about Aston making him sleep next to a supposedly disconnected gas stove, and that he hasn't got a clock in his room. All of them quite trivial things but in doing so, the two of them, Mick and Davies are relating to each other. By bitching together about Aston and seeing that they get along better together than they do when Aston is about, Pinter is showing how they relate to each other. By showing is that the two of them are able to get along and consequently capable of relating to each other. There are other examples of this, for example, on the other extreme there is the later part of Act three, where there is just Davies and Aston alone. In this part, there is conflict between the two of them constantly. He moans that it's cold, and that Aston is completely mad and should never have been let out. The conflict here, shows us that the two of them cannot relate to each other except in argument and consequently don't get along. This play clearly shows us the simple use of language which Pinter uses to allow the audience to understand how the characters relate to each other. However, one of the other plays I am studying, *The Dwarfs* has a much more complex system. In this play, there is conflict between all three of the characters, Len Mark and Pete. At certain points in the play, there is a time when the characters are talking about the other, i.e. Len and Pete talking about Mark, Mark and Pete talking about Len or Len and Mark talking about Pete. For example, when Len and Pete are talking, Pete tells Len that although he himself knows how to handle Mark, and can put up with him, he can't be doing Len any good. On the other hand, when Len and Mark are talking, Mark tells Len he spends too much time with Pete. Having said this, showing that they all obviously bitch and think little of each other when one is not with them, they all seem to get on very well. So although Pinter is showing us that through the conflict they have when there are two of them alone the three of them are not able to relate to each other.

However this is not so. It goes further because through showing the audience how the characters can relate to each other, we are also shown how insecure they are because they do not know whether they like or trust each other or not, yet they all get along.

Having shown two different methods by which Pinter uses to show how the characters relate to each other, and what the conflict between them tells the audience, I now intend to conclude the essay.

Having established a result in each stage, I now intend to draw a conclusion from each one. The first area I studied, which was examining the importance of stage setting, i.e. scenery, props and scene changes had quite an interesting outcome. It appears that Pinter makes a great use of the stage, not just as an area to set his plays in, but he actually takes advantage of it in many ways. Pinter makes great use of all props, providing a detailed description of what the stage should look like. He uses props for different things, starting off a conversation, giving characters something to do, indicating their personality and so on, and even when a prop is merely standing on its own, it is often brought into discussion, so nothing is left. Basically Pinter makes use of everything.

In the second area of study, where I looked at the insecurity of the characters, I found that Pinter again uses props in order of showing the characters insecurity, and to show how one character relates to another and by showing the insecurity of one character, he can show the differences between the others.

Finally, I studied how characters relate to each other, through their conflict, but getting along with each other but also doing copious amounts of bitching behind each others backs, and showing that the two who are complaining are in fact relating to each other – through conflict.

All in all, a combination of studies shows us that Pinters two main weapons in his plays are first, obviously language and characters. Using these he sets the scene and tells us about each character, and the story. Second, he uses props, scenery and scene changes a great deal in order of showing a characters personality or insecurity to open scenes with, to give characters something to do, but generally, no prop is useless or wasted. He makes use of all available props in order of making his plays exciting, interesting, thought provoking, challenging and most of all, intriguing.

This candidate appears to have an interest in Pinter and is able to make reference to several plays. From time to time there is some awareness of characters and situations and the candidate has thought about both the effects of the stage directions and the interactions of the characters. Beyond that, however, there is not a great deal that one can say about the positive achievement of the candidate in this essay. First of all the title is not addressed. It seems clear that the candidate has worked hard to try to create a logical and clear structure and to follow that structure with sufficient pointers to let the reader know where he is going next. The structure of the essay, however, does not relate in any clear or direct way to the title itself. 'Poetic' is not dealt with at all. Presumably 'images' is seen in terms of stage setting and props, but this is never clarified during the essay. What the phrase 'reality of life' might mean is never overtly addressed. The essay, therefore, remains as an essay on Pinter's stage directions and the interactions of some of his characters, but we do not discover the intention, purpose or effects of these, except in the broadest terms.

This particular essay raises the issue of length and underlines for us the absurdity of considering length alone as a means of assessment. A simple word count of this essay shows that it is certainly 'long enough', but the student writes the same thing over and over again. Were the matter of the essay, germane to the title, to be written out only once, it would be seen that the essay is very short indeed and that there is little to reward by way of positive achievement.

A further problem this candidate has is that the more he writes about any particular scene or part of the plays, the less we are convinced about his understanding. While much of the writing is very general indeed, where there is an attempt to expand one becomes doubtful whether he has taken the material on any but the most literal plane.

Lacking in argument and precise indications of what the writer is achieving in his plays, this essay has not reached A level standard. The assessment decision that needs to be made is whether there is sufficient understanding shown of the plot, situations and characters to warrant an N grade or whether the essay falls into the Fail bracket. Given the paucity of material and argument which actually addresses the task that he has set himself, we feel that this essay does not quite reach the N standard and in AEB terms warrants a mark of 16 out of 60.

EXAMPLE 7

Task

'A View to Death'. *A Comparison of* Where Angels Fear to Tread *and* A Room with a View.

E. M. Forster, while not one of the giants of the century, is nevertheless a novelist of considerable interest and importance, in spite of the fact that he only wrote six novels. In these novels Forster deals in a perceptive and illuminating way with the problem of human relationships set against an increasingly changing society and where clashes of culture are increasingly apparent.

A Room with a View exemplifies to some extent both these trends. It is a novel that can be seen in two sections, the first section with the background setting of Italy, but an Italy that is instinctively 'English', as exemplified in the fact that the 'Pension Bertolini' has not quite captured the essence of native Italy, but has through its 'cockney' signora caught the spirit of an English hotel with,

> Portraits of the Late Queen and Poet Laureate that hung behind the English people heavily framed, at the Notice of the English church Rev Cuthbert Edgar Oxon.

This background is, therefore, a clear indication that Italy is not the presiding influence over the relationship between characters as in *Where Angels Fear to Tread*, but merely a somewhat passive background upon which English people can meet and in doing so make an impact upon each other. Nevertheless, Italy's landscape does exert some influence upon the moods of the characters, its function is not totally passive. The romance between George and Lucy is able to begin amongst the field of violets that create a romantic setting which frees George's feelings for Lucy,

> He saw radiant joy in her face, he saw the flowers beat up against her dress in blue waves. The bushes above them closed. He stepped quickly forward and kissed her.

The visit to Santa Croce allows Mr Emerson and Cuthburt Edgar to meet and express their differing ideals, which I feel has a strong influence upon the way each character is judged throughout the remainder of the book. Mr Edgar believes that Santa Croce was built by 'faith in the full flavour of medievalism' whereas Mr Emerson blatantly disagrees,

> No, remember nothing of the sort. Built by faith indeed! That simply means the workmen weren't paid properly.

It is clear that Mr Emerson is very forthright and down to earth in his views and this has a considerable effect on Lucy and George's eventual happiness.

Forster's description of Italy and of the 'Pension Bertolini', also allows the mixing of different walks of life, which may not have been possible in the context of an English setting. Both middle and lower classes mix together, the Emersons have connections with the railway and are therefore seen to be quite different in manners and character when compared to the wealthy classes. Mr Emerson's honesty is seen as an embarrassment to Lucy and to Miss Bartlett, when over dinner he quite bluntly offers them the room with a view.

> 'What I mean is,' he continued, 'is that you can have our rooms, and we'll have yours. We'll change.'

Even Mr Beebe, quite literal in terms of the starched middle classes finds it 'difficult to understand people who speak the truth.'

England is the setting for the second part of the book, a small quaint village called 'Summer Street'. This section of the novel begins with the title 'Medievalism' and this word summarizes almost every apsect of Cecil Vyse, a young man of extreme aesthetic tastes who is to marry Lucy. He epitomizes Forster's 'flat' character and he is completely untouched by human passion and appears to be quite weary. He forms a stark contrast to George Emerson, who symbolises life, youthful vigour and passion. Their differences in character are perhaps highlighted most significantly in their desires for Lucy. Cecil sees Lucy in terms of a work of art, more specifically a 'Leanardo' and his attempt at embracing her is an utter disaster,

> As he touched her, his gold pince-nez became dislodged and was flattened between them.
> Such was his embrace. He considered with truth, that it had been a failure. Passion should believe itself irresistible.

However, George is overwhelmed by passion and desire for Lucy as shown in his quite spontaneous unashamed embraces,

> George who loved passionately must blunder against her in the narrow path.
> No – she gasped, for the second time was kissed by him.

Consequently, it can be said that George is an optimist and is always looking forward to the future whereas Cecil is trapped in the past, locked in 'Medievalism', with not the slighest idea on how to change his 'conventional' nature. Philip Herreton, one of the main protagonists in *Where Angels Fear to Tread* can be seen in a similar 'light' to Cecil, as both appear to have aesthetic tastes. Cecils is for Lucy whereas Philip's is for both Italy and to some extent Caroline Abbott whom, while washing Gino's baby appears as the vision of the 'virgin and child'. Philip, however, manages to unwrap himself from this outlook on life and is then able to understand himself and the pretenshous conventions of an urban society. Cecil, however 'wraps' himself 'in art' and his character consequently remains a symbol of 'anti-life'.

Where Angels Fear to Tread is quite different in structure when compared with *A Room with a View.* It is a novel which describes the way place can affect people. It shows how places cause both changes in human relationships and in people's characters. The setting of *Where Angels Fear to Tread* also uses two settings, that of England and Italy, the English background being that of Sawston. In Sawston the middle classes are seen to dominate the social scene and in contrast to this English setting a town in Tuscany called Monteriano is used. These two places are connected by four characters and by four journeys which are made throughout the course of the novel. Therefore, the extremes of Sawston society is joined with those of Monteriano.

The first journey is made by Lilia, a flighty woman who is subconsciously hoping to escape the claustrophobic values that preside in Sawston. She is accompanied by a chaperone in the shape of Miss Abbott. The novel opens with all of the main protagonists on the station waving Lilia goodbye and thus the action begins. Philip Herreton has had experience of society in Monteriano and believes he knows the Italian desposition extremely well. He therefore feels obliged to give Lilia advice on her departure.

> 'Remember,' he concluded, 'that it is only by going off track that you get to know the country. And don't let me beg you, go with that awful tourist idea that Italy's only a museum of antiques and art home and understand the Italians.'

Lilia, quite literally takes Philip's advice and falls in love with a native of Monteriano. Gino, Monteriano and its society can be seen as symbols of each other, in the same way Sawston and Mrs Herriton reflect the values of middle class wit and intellect. Both Gino and Mrs Herriton seem to have been conditioned by their own individual society to the extent that they themselves are not conscious of the fact. However, they are seen in complete contrast to one another. Mrs Herreton has been moulded into a part of Sawston and like Sawston had very little identity of her own. Her family esteem is very important to her. This is shown by the fact that she cannot bear to think of Lilia's child being educated in Italy or her granddaughter Irma letting the family's reputation down by saying 'boat' instead of 'ship' and in effect sounding common.

Mrs Herriton's feelings for anyone are concealed. It is evident that she has no compassion, unlike Gino who reflects the values of Monteriano. Monteriano's history is steeped in violence and has an aray of traditions which has meant that the present society sees the man presiding over the women. Also, because of its history Monteriano has become a close community. The man is the head of the family and must be seen in command as shown in the novel when Lilia wants to take a walk and go out alone,

> It would have been well if he'd have been as strict over his own behaviour as he was over hers. But the incongruity never occurred to him for a moment. His morality was that of the average Latin, and he was placed in the position of a gentleman. He did not see why he should behave as such.

Sawston, on the other hand symbolises English middle class values and is very much a superficial society in the respect that coffee mornings and church functions are of great importance to its inhabitants although there is a lack of true communication. Lilia attempts to take this social aspect of Sawston society to Monteriano,

> Most excellent advice and I thank you for it. But she wishes to give tea-parties – men and women together whom she had never seen.

In Monteriano personal feelings are shown freely in an open and honest manner. Philip and Caroline and even for a while Harriet change. They are able to escape from the values of Sawston. Caroline and Philip become conscious of the 'idleness, the stupidity, the respectability' it upholds.

The endings of both *Where Angels Fear to Tread* and *A Room with a View* appear to parallel each other in that both end positively, although I feel it is possible to regard the ending of *Where Angels Fear to Tread* as unconventional. Harriet kidnaps Gino's baby which subsequently dies in a coach accident and Philip as a consequence of this tragedy is left to break the news to a heartbroken father. Moreover, Gino is so overwrought and disturbed emotionally by the bitter news that he attacks Philip and in doing so attempts to kill him,

> 'Help! Help!' moaned Philip his body suffered too much for Gino . . . 'Oh the foul devil!' he murmured 'kill him! kill him for me.'

However, this miserable series of events is counteracted by a rather optimistic outlook for Caroline Abbotts' and Philip's future. Their lives all changed by the social climate of Italy. Philip is able to see the 'petty unselfishness' of Sawston society, that he had in the past not been so aware of. He is, by the end of the book, able to live without his despotic mother and has learned something of himself, about his completely passive and uninvolved attitude to life,

> You look on life as a spectacle; you don't enter it. You don't find anything funny or beautiful.

Caroline Abbott returns to Sawston a changed person. She is now capable of feeling that her life is of importance and she is not just a nonentity she felt she had been in the past. Philip, at the beginning of the novel sums up how Caroline was seen by the inhabitants of Sawston,

> She was good, quiet, dull and aimiable . . . there was nothing in her manner to suggest the fire of youth . . . her pleasant pallid face, bent on some respectable charity.

Therefore, it could be said that both these characters by the end of *Where Angels Fear to Tread* are transformed. Philip and Caroline are not only able to understand themselves but others who lack 'passion' and have become locked into the particular standards that a society expects.

The happy ending of *A Room with a View* reinforces the main themes and specific aims that Forster had intended to highlight in the novel. In fact it could be said that the ending of *A Room with a View* emphasises the 'holiness of direct desire' which Lucy feels. By the last chapter, she has admitted to herself and others her real feelings for George and Cecil and as a consequence she is able to begin a new life, away from the destructive domain of 'Medievalism' which Lucy may have become tangled up in if she had married Mr Vyse. However, it could be said that the build up to the end of the novel is a 'muddle'. Lucy is seen to deceive herself, she does manage to break up her engagement with Cecil, but feels that a trip to Greece with the Miss Alans will be her only escape from her confused desposition and 'Summer Street'.

> 'She must spare me!' cried Lucy, in growing excitement. 'I simply must go away. I have to.' She ran her fingers through her hair. 'Don't you see that I have to go away? I didn't realise at the time – and of course I want to see Constantinople particularly'.

Lucy 'Lies' to Cecil, Mr Beebe and Mr Emerson up to the point when she realises that she must face her desires. Mr Emerson helps clear her jumbled thoughts by his absolute truthfulness. His marriage to Lucy is straight forward and I feel indicates his whole outlook on life, 'We fight for more than love or pleasure, there is truth'.

The closing scene of the novel depicts Lucy and George looking through the window of their room in Italy. They are newly married and evidently in love, both have a chance of a new beginning. Moreover, Lucy is able to cast aside the formalities and 'Medievalism' society has expected and as a consequence she is able to begin to appreciate the meaning of love and absolute truth in herself. I feel that this may in effect, lead her to a much deeper understanding of the human spirit, which her past had not allowed,

> Youth enwrapped them; the song of Phaethon announced passion requited, love attained. But they were conscious of a love more mysterious than this.

Although the endings of the novels *A Room with a View* and *Where Angels Fear to Tread* are in contrast to each other, they can also be seen to have a similarity, that of the development of character through the interaction with people or places. The differing structures of the novels also emphasise the common themes shared between *Where Angels Fear to Tread* and *A Room with a View*.

Italy and England are the most important devices when contemplating the changes in character of Philip and Caroline and to some extent Harriet, who is seen to be somewhat hysterical and almost mad after the coaching incident,

> 'I stole it! I and the idiot – no-one was there' she burst out laughing.

The Italian landscape allows the characters to release their emotions and express themselves in an open manner, whereas in England, their feelings are seen to be vulgar.

In *A Room with a View* the conflict between different philosophies and ideologies are seen to be the most significant factor when considering a character and its development. Mr Emerson, is perhaps the most important attributor to these changes in Lucy, encompassing his own values he manages to convince Lucy that her love should not be hidden behind a wall of social conformities but in fact her feeling should be expressed in an honest and truthful manner,

> He gave her a sense of deities reconciled, a feeling that, in gaining the man she loves, she would gain something for the whole world . . . It was as if he had made her see the whole of everything at once.

Lucy, as a consequence is released from the pointless clutches of Cecil and 'Medievalism' and becomes what seems to be the epitome of Forster's 'Round' character. She is therefore able to live with 'passion' and the full knowledge of her desires.

It is quite apparent that both novels offer an outlook on middle class Georgian society of the time. Forster describes, through his writing the type of traditions which were expected of the time. One expectation of society was that a woman should not travel alone but at all times be seen to be accompanied by a chaperone. I felt that the chaperones not only served the purpose of reinforcing middle class expectations but can also be seen to be very important characters in the two novels in as far as either directly or indirectly influencing Lucy and Lilia. Both Miss Abbott and Miss Bartlett exert some type of restraint over the activities and desires of the two women. Miss Bartlett is seen as the supresser of Lucy's desires. She watches the incident which occurs between Lucy and George in the field of violets and worries about the moral dilemma that could develop as a consequence of this romantic outburst,

> 'I have been a failure', said Miss Bartlett, as she struggled with the straps of Lucy's trunk instead of strapping her own. 'Failed to make you happy; Failed in my duty to your mother. She has been so generous to me; I shall never face her again after this disaster.'

In fact Miss Bartlett decides that Lucy and herself should leave for Rome, as Miss Bartlett appears determined that Lucy should not develop an affection for George. Her character is seen as 'flat' and she appears to be very much like Cecil in her restrained attitudes to passion and profound desire.

However, her totally unsympathetic nature is tarnished at the end of the play, and I felt as though she believed deeply in her soul that youthful passion should win against the constraints of the middle classes. It is possible that she arranged Lucy's meeting with Mr Emerson and perhaps in the past had been touched by human passion. Lucy and George discuss this idea at the very end of the novel,

> 'How like Charlotte to undo her work by a feeble muddle at the last moment.' But something in the dying evening, in the roar of the river, in their very embrace, warned them that her words fell short of life, and George whispered: 'Or did she mean it?'

Therefore, Miss Bartlett can be seen as an instigator in creating Lucy's future happiness, yet for the majority of the novel she appears as a human barrier between Lucy's real desires for George.

Caroline Abbott is in many ways different from Miss Bartlett. At first she seemed a feeble character unable to control the flighty antics of an older woman,

> But Lilia was already calling to Miss Abbott, a tall, grave, rather nice looking young lady who was conducting her adieus in a rather more decorous manner on the platform. 'Caroline, my Caroline! Jump in, or your chaperon will go off without you.'

However, further into the novel it is apparent that Caroline Abbott is not just a background character used as a way of reinforcing the expectations of Sawston society, in particularly the idea that women should not travel alone. In fact Caroline Abbott appears to become a 'round' character with much more depth and understanding than perhaps any other character in *Where Angels Fear to Tread*. Perhaps the turning point of Caroline Abbott's character of a rather nervous and stupid chaperone is on the train journey to London where a totally new dimension of her character is revealed to both the reader and to Philip. She tells Philip that she did not merely allow Lilia's marriage to Gino but that she had initiated it,

> And Gino, I thought was splendid, and young and strong not only in body, and sincere as the day. If they wanted to marry, why shouldn't they do so! Why shouldn't she break with the deadening life where she had got into a groove'.

It is also evident that she dislikes the matriarchal society that Sawston epitomises and also its 'stupidity'. Philip is too intelligent a character to be satisfied with Sawston, as shown from the beginning his aesthetic tastes are indeed those that lead him to explore Italy,

> And Philip, whom the idea of Italy always intoxicated, had started again, telling her of the supreme moments of her coming journey – the Campanile of Airolo, which would burst on her when she emerged from the St Gottherd tunnel, presaging the future.

His ideas and experience from past visits to Italy have transformed his outlook of Sawston values, although he has felt from these excursions that he can do nothing to change this passionless society.

> All the energies and enthusiasms of a rather friendless life had passed into the championship of beauty.
> In a short time it was over. Nothing had happened either in Sawston or within himself.

However, although he has been, to some extent, set free from Sawston society by his visits, I feel that he is still very much a victim of its values and moreover a victim at the disposal of his mother. As shown at its most absolute in his immediate packing for Italy, upon his mothers request.

> So Philip receives with the news that he must start in half an hour for Monteriano.

Philip, however, through his experiences in Italy is able to take part in life and is subsequently able to fall in love in Italy, although his love can in some respects be seen to parallel Cecil's for Lucy,

So they were when Philip entered, and saw, to all intents and purposes, the Virgin and Child, with Donor.

As a woman Lucy Honeychurch has a totally different role from Philip. This could quite possibly explain that while she is fighting for her own recognizable individuality the obsicales she faces and the manner in which she expresses herself are in many ways totally different from Philip in *Where Angels Fear to Tread*. Lucy is instinctively a young women in a society where her own conditioning has meant that her predjuices are those that are against freeing herself. She has to fight not one character, as Philip does, but has to fight a group of people from Cecil to the quite liberal Mr Beebe.

Although, it could be said that Lucy's status in society is to some respects to her advantage. She is able to express her thoughts in some subjects fully. Lucy is also free of responsibilities and anxities. On the other hand, Philip has to hide his thoughts from the social circle that exists within Sawston. Philip is also seen to have responsibilities and has to act in a mature manner. Lucy, however, has to be seen by society as innocent and as a consequence has to contend with a chaperone for want of travel and experience.

It is through Lucy that some of the minor themes in *A Room with a View* are highlighted, those of music and art. Lucy, also has aesthetic tastes although they are not as severe as Cecils. It is possible to suggest that Lucy's judgement of character is signalled through her choice of music. She plays Shuman to the Vyses and this appears to parallel their weariness and dry 'wit'. On another occasion she plays Gluck Amide, it reflects her mood on Georges arrival in Summer Street.

It seems ironic that Lucy's mother, Mrs Honeychurch dislikes Lucy's playing as she feels it makes her daughter foolish and impractical, perhaps symbolizing the type of claustrophobic air that existed in the middle class society of the time.

In conclusion I enjoyed both *Where Angels Fear to Tread* and *A Room with a View* and it appears that both novels have a similarity that is echoed throughout E. M. Forster's novels, that the development of character can be seen through the interaction and connection of people and place.

This essay is extremely problematic. If one forgets all about a particular task and reads the bits of it one by one, then one realises that this candidate has some critical ability and that she makes some thoughtful and interesting comparisons and contrasts between characters, both within the two novels and between them. She has developed a personal response to the novels and has managed to generate some ideas about the effect of Forster's various juxtapositions and contrasts. However, there remain some fundamental problems with this piece which make it look like a draft of material which still needs to be sorted rather than a final product. First of all, the title is far from helpful. We never discover the significance of 'A View to Death'; indeed it is never mentioned, and about halfway through the essay we give up looking for its significance altogether. Secondly, the essay gets off to a dreadful start with apparently several different beginnings one after another, none of which illuminates what is to follow. The candidate has great difficulty in putting any of her insights into a conceptualised frame which we realise at the end when the conclusion to the essay is as unhelpful in trying to define a focus as the beginning. However, we do realise at the end what the candidate thought her main thread was – the effect of place on the characters and how changes in place have highlighted their conflicts and changes in behaviour. Overlying this main thread is another – that of 'flat' and 'round' characters.

The candidate includes a lot of detail in the essay and uses many quotations, although these are never analysed and some of them sit rather uneasily in their context. Although there are some interesting and thoughtful parts to the essay, the whole does not cohere at all and the candidate does not display the necessary skills of creating and developing an argument. It is curious that there are so many inaccuracies in the quotations which she uses, leading one to speculate whether this version was a hurried final version done at the last moment after a great deal of time spent on gathering materials. There is certainly a fundamental fault in structure and organisation as well as the primary fault in failing to achieve a comprehensible focus. As the original marker noted:

> You have gathered together a great deal of information but unfortunately your essay, as a whole, seems to lack direction. You do not seem to know *what* you feel about Forster's writing; consequently there is no *central* thesis permeating your essay.

In assessing this essay, one has to balance the positive merits – involvement with and close knowledge of the text; some detailed comparisons and contrasts between characters; moments of personal critical response to the material; the ability to range through the two texts for illustrative material; awareness of the function of the different settings – with the less successful aspects – the failure to conceptualise; a rambling structure; inaccuracy in detail and in supporting material; inordinate length and some repetition; the lack of a central argument or focus. While the essay does not fulfil the descriptors for the typical E grade essay it does combine the descriptions in the N grade and the D grade and thus one arrives here at a mark in the E grade. In AEB 660 terms a mark of 26 would be appropriate.

7

NON-FICTION

The original intention of the compulsory inclusion of a non-fiction text within the framework of AEB 660 was to broaden students' field of study and to enable them to consider what might by meant by the term 'literature' in the context of a two-year A level course. Many different approaches have been adopted with many different kinds of text for this particular element of the course. Among the variety of texts used as the basis for this work are the following:

- biography
- autobiography
- travel writing
- diaries
- letters
- works of criticism
- journalism
- inter-disciplinary writing (for example, *Ways of Seeing*)
- accounts of experience.

Perhaps because this is an unfamiliar and innovatory area in an A level Literature syllabus, teachers seem to find it poses them with more problems of choice of text and task construction than other aspects of AEB 660.

The final choice of text can be helped by testing possibilities against the syllabus Objectives, and against the key questions posed at the end of Chapter 2. It can also be made easier if the course as a whole has been constructed with certain concepts in mind – such as genres of text, or the processes of writing, or an attempt to define what is meant by 'literature', or ways of behaving as a reader.

Whatever text is selected from a very wide range of possibilities, the construction of tasks is often bedevilled by the feeling that the text must be treated as 'literature', and approached in similar ways using a similar set of critical approaches. This is likely to result in topics which focus on form and style, and to deny the fact that, in comparison with novels, plays or poems, issues relating to purpose and audience are likely to be far more pertinent and central to non-fiction. An invitation to consider the ideas and content of a non-fiction text should, however, lead into a discussion of form and style as an integral part of that consideration. Doing this might even feed back into other parts of the course and help students to a fuller understanding of how content and form interrelate in more 'literary' works.

It is worth thinking quite hard about the opportunities which the non-fiction text offers, which extend or differ from those presented by the other texts studied for coursework. If it is paired or clustered with other related texts, then the opportunities for reflection on a wider reading experience, or on differing representations of experience, are extended. If students are given the freedom to identify and base their own writing on aspects of the text which interest them most, then the diversity of reader response can be acknowledged and encouraged. Through the study of non-fiction the 'well-considered personal response' of syllabus Objective 5 can be redefined to extend beyond the expression of personal emotions and feelings in response to fiction, drama or poetry into a reflective consideration of the student's own experience and that of others.

Some centres use this option to allow their students to select any work of non-fiction of their own choice (sometimes from an extensive list of suggestions), and then to attempt one or more of a range of assignments based upon this reading. Such an approach can lead to some worthwhile group presentations and collaborative learning as well as to group decisions about grounds for description, criticism and evaluation.

Many centres have attempted to get students to think particularly about the content of the text and then to consider whether the same kind of criteria are and should be used for the appreciation of a non-fiction text as for any other. The examples which follow attempt to broaden the traditional scope of A level English Literature study: one by making a comparison between text and film, and another by making comparisons with journalism. While these tasks all arose from the teaching, as always, the task itself did not necessarily reflect all the work that had gone into the students' learning about different aspects of these texts. We have said before, and it is worth repeating here, that when the task is framed in such a way as to afford a comparison or contrast with other works, or to use methodologies sometimes adopted in other disciplines, then it is vital for the student to be as confident in that other mode as he or she is in the literary one. Thus if a comparison is to be made between a written text and a film, then it is essential for the differences between the genres to be at the front of the student's mind. Similarly, if the comparison is with journalism, then some awareness of the nature of journalism is necessary for the interplay to be fruitful. Other approaches, however, depend more fully on the context of the student's own personal experience and allow for a more mature reflection on the issue being discussed or described in the text. It is this kind of task which forms our third example in this section.

EXAMPLE 8

Task

How far does John Hersey's Hiroshima *use journalistic technique?*

John Hersey, an American journalist, wrote the book *Hiroshima*, a year after the atomic bomb was dropped onto the Japanese city of Hiroshima on 6th August 1945. 100,000 people perished and those who miraculously survived suffered terrible losses and after effects. Hersey's book tells the harrowing stories of six men and women who managed to survive. Forty years later Hersey added an extra chapter to the book entitled 'The Aftermath' where one is able to meet the same six people again and assess how the bomb altered their lives.

The book *Hiroshima* contains many various forms of journalistic techniques usually found in a newspaper, these include sensationalism, humanising of horror and slap dash construction, all are illustrated below.

Hersey introduced one to the characters by writing an indepth description of their appearance, their lifestyle and job and exactly what they were doing at the time of the explosion.

Mr Tanimato – '. . . the prominence of the frontal bones just above his eyebrows and the smallness of his moustache, mouth and chin gave him a strange, old-young look, boyish and yet wise, weak and yet fiery.'

Such a lengthy description can hardly be classed as necessary to the events of August 1945, but one does feel that one knows a lot about the people involved. This is clearly what Hersey wishes us to feel.

Dr Masakazu Fujii was settling down crosslegged to read the Osaki Asahi on the porch of his private hospital.

This is an example of what Hersey writes in order to tell one where each person was before the bomb exploded. The first few chapters of *Hiroshima* are full of other such incidents when Hersey manages to humanise the horror and bring the deaths and suffering of the people of all ages and many nationalities to life.

Sensationalism is another major journalistic technique that Hersey uses, particularly in Chapter Three with reference to the horrific injuries suffered by the people of Hiroshima.

> . . . took a woman by the hands, but her skin slipped off in huge, glovelike pieces.

Hersey couldn't have found a better description to describe the horror, followed by

> . . . twenty men, . . . all in exactly the same nightmarish state: their faces were wholly burned, their eyesockets were hollow, the fluid from their melted eyes had run down their cheeks.

The line is blunt and straightforward, clearly written to shock which is another journalistic technique intended to draw a persons interest.

The use of facts within the book again illustrates journalistic technique. Hersey uses facts in various forms, the first one is introduced to us when he tells one about the six people the book follows. He recounts a brief history, of each person, descriptions of their jobs, family, ages and then goes on to describe exactly where they were and what they were doing when the bomb was dropped.

> Miss Tashiko Sasaki, a clerk in the personnel department of the East Asia Tin Works, had just sat down in the plant office and was turning her head to speak to the girl at the next desk.

> (the plant was 1,600 yards from the centre).

Hersey also included facts about other incidents: when the atomic bomb was used, including the attack on Nagasaki and tests carried out by countries of the world. These facts are made prominent as they are printed in italics, are short and state simply the date and what took place.

> On July 1, 1946, before the first anniversary of the bombing the United States had tested an atomic bomb at Bikini Atoll.
> In October 1952, Great Britain conducted its first test of an atomic bomb and the United States its first of a hydrogen bomb.

Hersey makes no comments, gives no further details and no elaboration on what took place and the future repercussions.

The frequent use of rhetorical points throughout the book is also a trademark of newspaper journalists. Hersey simply states what happens but makes no comment, perhaps because of his requirements as a journalist to remain unbiass where possible.

> . . . even if they had known the truth, most of them were . . . too weary or too badly hurt to care that they were the objects of the first great experiments in the use of atomic power . . . no country except the United States, with its . . . willingness to throw two billion gold dollars into an important wartime gamble could possibly have developed.

The above quote is written to show the differences between the Japanese people of Hiroshima who don't know and don't care what happened to them, compared to the coldness of the United States who feels that it is able to spend so much money on an experiment, that would inevitably lead to terrible destruction and loss of life. Hersey simply leaves one to make their own mind up.

Lastly one arrives at the construction of the book, journalists tend to be very slapdash when putting pieces of work together. *Hiroshima* consists of five chapters, the titles of which could be the titles that newspaper journalists use to break their work up with, examples include 'A Noiseless Flash' and 'The Fire'. Each chapter includes sections on the individual characters, changing from one to the other. This is good in that it means that one is aware of what is happening to the various people at a similar time. However it can also be criticised because one can lose track of which character is which, a problem not improved because of the people's names. The exception to this form of construction is the final chapter 'The Aftermath', Hersey splits the characters up and we learn what has happened to them over the last forty years individually. The drawback to this is simply that Hersey's account is at times rather long and one can lose track of what is taking place, the most prominent example being that of Mr Tanimoto. One learns about his ideas for a peace centre, how he travels around America lecturing and now at the age of seventy,

> He was slowing down a bit. His memory, like the world's was getting spotty.

Hiroshima is a moving book about a terrible event that will have repercussions. Hersey manages to shock and provoke one into questioning the ethics behind the use of such a weapon as the atomic bomb. One of the most shocking things that one finds in the book is the attitude of the leaders to the explosion. The President of the United States stated 'That bomb had more power than twenty thousand tons of TNT . . . The Emperor of Japan said that the people had made a whole hearted sacrifice for the everlasting peace of the world.' A study of the book reveals the enormous extent to which Hersey uses journalistic technique in its many forms. Due to his consistent use of these techniques such as sensationalism and slapdash construction the book may well have been a failure, however his clever use of six major characters makes the book interesting and brings the horror alive to us in a way that simple facts could never do. Therefore I believe that Hersey's use of journalistic technique on the whole very successful, its downfall being that the book is in parts very simple where it may well have needed more detail and very detailed where a simple fact could have replaced what was written. Each of the six major characters were fairly lucky but as Hersey writes,

> . . . each knows that in the act of survival he lived a dozen lives and saw more death than he ever thought he would see. At the time, none of them knows anything.

In this instance we shall consider the wording of the task alongside the student's response. This is the kind of task often seen in examination papers with its 'How far' and its mention of 'technique'. Indeed, it is difficult to imagine just what sort of response was expected to 'How far', given the conditions of coursework where all aspects of a given title can be considered and treated. Were this a timed examination piece, however, the understanding would be that anyone attempting the topic could do no more than begin to suggest some sort of quantitative working hypothesis. Our candidate has considerable difficulty with this title. She certainly begins with the identification of several techniques which she feels to be journalistic and provides examples of them, yet having done this she first of all illustrates not the use of these techniques but rather what Hersey does in his use of elaborate descriptions. She is more direct in her comments on sensationalism and the use of facts, although she does not grapple fully with the impact of these facts or their intention in the book. As she considers structure she makes some extraordinary assertions like 'journalists tend to be very slapdash when putting pieces of work together'. This appears to be clear evidence of the candidate's reluctance to use specific examples of journalism from which to draw out her characteristics; it is hard to believe that she really does feel that all journalism is slapdash and she certainly does not attempt to justify her assertion. Had she thought as carefully about journalism as she has thought about *Hiroshima* then she would have enabled herself to make some rather more sophisticated comments. One of the problems she experiences is that once her categories have been established the illustration becomes somewhat formulaic; examples are given but their intention and effect is often neglected. In her response, the candidate shows some understanding of the text and is able to provide apt examples of several of the characteristics she identifies. She does not, however, answer the question of 'How far?'. The task she has attempted is more like the following:

> Identify some features of journalism and show how Hersey uses these techniques in his book. Go on to explore your own response to the way he writes, indicating how successful you feel his writing to be.

This less prescriptive wording would have enabled the candidate to fulfil more precisely what she had been asked to do. Indeed, at the end of the essay the candidate reveals that she thinks that her task has been the one I have suggested, not the one she was given. This raises the fundamental importance of the precise wording of the task and of the need to provide constructs which enable students to frame their responses to the texts within the framework of the given words.

The candidate is able to identify some central preoccupations of the text and she is able to show her appreciation of the way it is written. Apart from failing to grasp or remember the 'How far?' of the title, she fulfils the rest of its demands adequately. The conclusion, however, indicates the lack of overall conceptualisation. There are some inherent contradictions in what is written which the candidate does not appear to notice. It is another example of the way in which a rather formulaic approach leads to statements which have not been fully thought about. Although she is not always confident in her general critical comments, her treatment of detail is sound and effective, showing the ability to move through the text to find suitable illustrative material. Her individual comments are more secure than her overall conceptualisation of the response. Overall, this work's uncertainty of stance and concepts leads to an award of a D grade and a mark of 7. The assessment is made problematic by the failure of the candidate to grasp the central significance in the title of the opening two words.

EXAMPLE 9

Task

Compare the film of I Know Why the Caged Bird Sings to Maya Angelou's autobiography. Does the film differ from the text in a way that radically affects the themes or atmosphere?

Maya Angelou's autobiography is not a light hearted story or a life filled with chapters of 'human interest' but a straightforward, enlightening and heart-rending account of her real life. There are definite atmospheres given to the reader through the book, that of terror during the rape, satisfaction at her new born child and confusion, pity but mainly anger at the racism shown rather more subtly in the book than the film. However because it is based on personal ideas, thoughts, triumphs and ambitions, the filming of the book would not be an easy undertaking.

Emotions of the characters are always a problem for actors to portray, but when those emotions either stem from a young girl or are seen from a young girl's viewpoint, for example she sometimes tries to assess how Momma is feeling, and this, along with her own thoughts and personal dreams make certain things differ, understandably in the film to the autobiography. One example which shows this difference is Maya's dream of being a white girl. When we read this in the book we are convinced this was a young child's real dream, but in the film due to the age of the actress and because she actually has to say her dream to an unbelieving brother, it comes across as a half-hearted, sarcastic joke which she no longer or indeed never had believed in.

Voice overs are a way of combating getting her thoughts across and these were used sparingly in the film, to good intent, for too many of them can cause it to be less of a film, more of a story book with pictures being read to you. One way they do try, which I thought did change the character of Maya slightly, was the argument between Momma and Maya in which everything Maya was thinking to herself in the book but would never dare to say to Momma, is stated by her bluntly and loudly to a Momma who now seems to have lost the battle. In the book she so graciously won. This makes Maya a more forthright child and a much stronger character than the child who's the main story early on in the autobiography.

The racism felt by Bailey Jr. and Maya is another problem to be coped with by the film makers. I think unfortunately they had to revert to the old, recognised symbol of the Ku Klucks clan. I think this drastically changes the whole affect of racism the book produces. The book uses more subtle ways, for instance the event with the dentist. This brought the racism down on a more personal basis, as did Maya's employee calling her Mary rather than the obvious 'white hate black'. The book is also alot fairer, Maya actually admits she didn't really know what a white child looked like and even though we may say they had a right to be the black people in the book are definitely more racist than they came across in the film.

An obvious change in the story line was the finishing of the film at the graduation. Where the book finishes on a more personal note, the film finishes on a more triumphant glorious note for the future of the blacks. Despite the fact that there were many events after the graduation, such as her first job as a tram conductor, that I believe to be important to the theme of her autobiography, I have to admit that this was a good way to end the film of *I Know Why the Caged Bird Sings.* We have to remember the film was made for the general public and as Maya is the main character she should always be in the limelight for the interest to be caught and kept, therefore it is understandable that at the graduation they allow Maya to make the speech that the head boy makes in the book. Therefore, this does again change the character very slightly of Maya, thus changing the atmosphere, from a day of hopeful anxiety of what the future holds to that of glorious anticipation.

I think also, it is a shame that they roll Louise into the character of Miss Flowers in the film. Maya says in the book that it was with Louise that she learned to be a girl after she so suddenly and early became a woman. This was an important turning point for Maya and her learning to be a 'girl' did not come across at all in the film.

The book is also more realistic about the presents Maya and Bailey Jr. first receive from their parents. Maya's principles are definitely clear in the film where she keeps nothing and ruins all her presents, to show the audience their obvious hate for the parents deserting them, however in the book Maya is a little more honest, and admits that the little girl who gets these surprise gifts secretly keeps the tea-set. Here she is allowed to show a little weakening in her character, but it seems that in the film Maya's gradual gaining of strength and hope, is ignored and she must be a strong principaled young lady almost from the start.

Maya's awkwardness, is, though, conveyed very well, with a long dangling armed and wonderfully wide eyed actress, the beginning scene of the book though of her not remembering the words to a poem is changed, to kill two birds at once by also showing Bailey's strength and her love for him, by Bailey standing in class and reading a poem.

A theme carried across most prominently by the book is shown in the title, 'I know why the caged bird sings'. It is that although Maya and her fellow negroes are caged, either by their colour or lifestyle, they still 'sing' and enjoy life. This is only put across in the film in the picnic scene and sadly the revival meetings in the church are missed out totally. Maybe the producers thought it unnecessary but those scenes lightened the story in the book and proved the people know how to 'enjoy' themselves and that there was some humour in their lives! It would also have shown how religious the negroes were, another theme not so prominent in the film.

Momma, strong, sturdy, unemotional, christian and straightforward. The character in the book that gives Maya strength if not comfort seemed only very slightly different in the film. Maybe Maya Angelou felt more understanding at the time of filming, for her but Momma came across as more sympathetic and sensitive in the film than one could imagine her being after descriptions in the book, which was also true of Uncle Willie. True he was noble and righteous to the last in both the book and film, but Maya talks of her and Bailey being scared of Uncle Willie and him threatening them in the book, which was thoughtfully omitted in the film making him more sad than angry. His humility at being hidden in the onions and potatoes is shown well and the atmosphere given in the book of anger, shame and feelings of being ridiculed are all clearly there in the film.

The actress playing Maya was excellent and the changes in Maya's character came across only through the lines she was given. Except perhaps, where the rape scene is concerned. In the book I was totally horrified and almost sick at the thought of Mr Freeman raping an eight year old child, however these feelings were not so intense when I watched the film. In that I felt more sympathy and anger for Maya and Mr Freeman. I think the change in atmosphere here was due, for me anyway, to the age of the actress playing Maya, the rape of a fifteen year, although horrifying is not as sickening as that of an eight year old child.

As for Mr Freeman, I was quite disgusted at the way the film portrayed him. In the book he was a strong, big, powerful man, created suddenly into a pathetic almost simple-minded, sad little wimp on film. This could be just their way of trying to justify his raping Maya, maybe she felt sorry for him after the 'holding time' – something also omitted from the film for fear of giving the impression Maya had encouraged him.

However, one thing that sticks in my mind for being extremely well done by the film makers was the scene of Joe Lewis fight on the radio. The tense atmosphere, the theme of their black man against all the whites, all came across as clearly as the book.

When comparing the film to the book, obviously things are going to have to be changed, but things such as Maya's character, the clu clucks clan, which have varied a great deal from the book, are they really necessary. After reading the book it is hard to judge the film on its own merit, however, when we remember that the film is not particularly a strong protest film, but a human interest story for ordinary people to watch and enjoy, these dramatic changes to events and characters seem to lessen somewhat.

The book on the other hand is making a definite point, published by Virago for a start and aimed to be read, and read again, not to be stored on a dusty bookshelf. However, it is also an autobiography and with the delicate blend of subtle racism and personal victories it gives across its points without dictating and tells a fascinating story of her life at the same time. In its own way, slightly different at times to the book, the film gives the same message, but allows an audience to sit back and enjoy and maybe not have to think about it as much as they would have the book.

Although some of the writing at the beginning is rather too general to communicate clearly, the candidate's approach of isolating problems facing the filmmaker is successful and shows some keen awareness of genre. Close attention to the comparison between film and book allows the candidate to produce some sharp insights, often expressed well, such as 'changing the atmosphere from a day of hopeful anxiety of what the future holds to that of a glorious anticipation'. The candidate also shows that she is aware of the nature of different audiences for the book and the film. The candidate throughout the piece is concerned to try to account for the differences and it is this focus which allows her to give a detailed and analytical approach to the task. The conclusion follows the discussion and argument, and suggests that the candidate has by the end been able to work towards an overall view of the film adaptation. Her examples are effective in making her points without becoming laboured or repetitive. It is curious that a writer with considerable perception, capable of analysis and insight, should have so much trouble about some of the simpler aspects of grammar, punctuation and syntax. This is a striking example of a student with relatively modest technical writing abilities being able to convey some critical and analytical ideas. She has clearly engaged fully with both film and book and her work deserves a B grade and a mark of 10.

EXAMPLE 10

Task

'Accept me for what I am and I'll accept you for what you're accepted as.' How has your study of Christopher Nolan's Under the Eye of the Clock *altered your perception of life for the disabled?*

Modern society, technologically advanced with a higher standard of living has done much to aid the disabled with mobility and education. Yet automatic prejudice against the disabled still exists, it takes many forms, and in one form or another almost everybody has displayed it. Such prejudice ranges from the malevolent ignorance of those who mock the disabled; to the discomfort felt by those who class themselves as 'normal' when faced with the disabled; and those who treat the disabled as sub-human imbeciles. Perhaps this springs from the difficulty of coming to terms with the massive misfortune which 'normal' people perceive that disabled people must endure. Many people feel guilt at their own good fortune. But Christopher Nolan's book dispels this air of gloom and depression surrounding disability – the accepted face of the disability. He goes far to humanise the disabled, revealing aspects of their lives which are normally ignored and establishing common links between the disabled and the 'normal' world.

Perhaps one of the most common pre-conceptions of the disabled, which I myself would admit to, is automatically assuming that the disabled are mentally retarded. This springs, in cases such as Christopher Nolan's, from the disabled person's inability to control their bodily functions. For a person who accepts themself as normal it is difficult to reconcile a person who dribbles and has muscle spasms or cannot control their face with someone who is capable of intellectual thought. Nolan conveys strongly through Joseph the deep misery and disillusionment he encountered because of this accepted view of the disabled.

> Some-one always vetoes his application, thought Joseph . . . someone normal; someone beautiful, someone administering the rusty mind's rules of yester-year.

This is one of the few moments of resentment at disabled people in *Under the Eye of the Clock*, and it is contagious, stimulating disgust and empathy. By writing the novel itself, Nolan dispels the view that the disabled are unintelligent. But by illustrating the damage caused by people accepting him 'for what he is accepted as', rather than for what he is he destroys in the reader any further ambiguous misconceptions. The strength of my reaction to such a young, intelligent boy being refused normal schools because 'crippled boyhood could not be hors d'oeuvred on the menu of a normal, flashy school' ensured that I would no longer think of the disabled as retarded as well, and it reinforced the message that the disabled cannot just be accepted as 'dross' to be ignored as they have been throughout history.

Once one accepts the intellectual normality of the disabled person the reader becomes aware of common aspects between the lives of the disabled and the able-bodied. Nolan takes great care in describing aspects of life and growing up with which the reader can identify. Once the gulf between the disabled and the 'normal' world is spanned, the reader realises there is no 'normal' world and it becomes much easier to accept the disabled.

Nolan often uses humourous episodes to display Joseph's normality, one such episode is when Joseph and his friend are playing with his wheelchair. His nervousness at his mother's reaction to the inevitable crash is easy to relate to. Everybody has erred as a child, living in fear of their parent's reaction. However, Nora's attitude is very touching and reminds us that Joseph is like any other child.

> Nothing happened because parents realise that boys have got to be boys despite being disabled.

One of the more common responses to the disabled is to ignore them in embarrassed discomfort, not wishing to acknowledge their disability. Yet such behaviour does not really consider the feelings of the disabled person for as Nolan illustrates it makes them even more self-conscious. From Joseph's introduction it is noticeable that certain actions prove embarrassing to Joseph. For example for Joseph to drink in public is a 'bold' feat, conveying his consciousness of his disability. I realised after reading *Under the Eye of the Clock* that the disabled person is just as embarrassed and frustrated by such involuntary actions like muscle spasm or unconscious dribbling as is the person watching.

> He saw how other people saw him but he wanted to show everyone how truly wrong they were.

This is a clear instance where Nolan shows his disillusionment that to many he is accepted as just a cripple, nothing beyond. Nolan does not always rely on melancholic examples to show his feelings about his disability, on the contrary he is light-hearted for the majority of the novel. Above all Nolan does not want the disabled to be viewed as resentful and sad at their misfortune. To avoid this he describes the good time he has enjoyed with his family and friends, rarely describing those times when he succumbs to self-pity. Particularly humourous is his friend's attitude towards those who will not accept Joseph.

> Ya can't beat sense into the bastards, they see themselves as normal and the assholes can't see further than their own noses.

The colloquial nature of the language shows the simple strength and sincerity of his friends convictions. It reflects that if such a normal, simplistic person can accept Joseph for what he is, then everybody ought to be able to do so.

These examples have certainly changed my attitude and no longer will I avoid their gaze in the mistaken belief that I am saving them from discomfort.

Although Christopher Nolan would not like his disability to be thought of as something abnormal, I still found myself struck by Joseph's bravery in overcoming his disability. The reader is constantly reminded of his struggle with his body just by reading his novel for Nolan describes the painstaking nature of the process of writing it. Even though the research of an expert and the advances of modern science speeded up his process, by a specially designed computer system, his body still created problems.

> Joseph waited for the green cursor to come to the required letter, but . . . his entire body froze rigid . . . The next time was the same and the next.

Not only does Joseph have to type each letter by waiting for a cursor to reach it, but he also has to battle his body to choose that letter. The frustration of missing a letter must be intense, and not many writers would have the skill and courage to write if it took minutes to write a sentence. The structure of the book conveys the arduous nature of Nolan's task, for each chapter comprises of short sections describing different activities in Joseph's life. This is because it takes so long for Joseph to write one section, that he has to break up his creative thought each day.

There are many other examples of Joseph's courage and perseverance, for example, his wish to go to school, facing the outside world on his own and his subsequent wish to attend university. These targets not only reflect the bravery of the disabled but also the difficulty in taking their place in the outside world. It shows their reliance on friends and family, particularly poignant because Joseph in *Under the Eye of the Clock* is unwilling to burden his family by carrying on his university study.

Perhaps one of the most important aspects of the novel is the help, support and love Joseph receives from his family. It is his mother who stands by Joseph when he realises his disability, reassuring him that his parents are not disappointed in him. Joseph vindicates their love and devotion through his achievements literary and otherwise. Yet Nolan has an important message to broadcast, in an attempt to change peoples perception of the disabled, especially the modern world's readiness to abort spastic babies. Nolan's emotional plea has changed my view on what I now see as an abuse of modern technology to 'play God'. I found myself deeply touched by Nolan's assertion that,

> . . . the spastic baby would ever be the soul which would never kill, maim breed falsehood or hate brotherhood. Why then does society fear the crippled child . . .?

After reading the novel my perception of those who were disabled had profoundly changed and I found myself admiring those whom I might previously have underestimated greatly. I found myself no longer pitying the disabled but wishing to support them, removing obstacles such as the intransigent and condescending people Joseph encounters. *Under the Eye of the Clock* gave me much to think about, especially the attitude of modern society to what is seen as less than perfect.

This task is particularly well framed to enable students to reflect on themselves in relation to the content of the text. This candidate structures his response carefully and thoughtfully in that he takes the various strands of the opening quotation and ties them neatly together. He spends time outlining his own response to the disabled both before and after he studied the text and it is clear that his own discoveries have allowed him to develop personally. The quotations from the text are well chosen and he knows the book well enough to be able to select telling and dramatic elements. The sections towards the end of the essay where he reflects on the structure of the text and its relationship to the disabled show particular insight and the concluding remarks tie the text and himself together very effectively. This is a well-written essay which is enjoyable to read, combining critical awareness with self-awareness and creating and maintaining a mood and tone which reflect the nature and position of the text itself. The candidate shows awareness of the intention and effect of the text, understanding of issues relating to the disabled and the ability to reflect and ponder on his own reactions. It is broad in scope but unfussy, worthy of a place at the bottom of the A grade, and a mark of 12.

8

CREATIVE EXTENSION

___

GCSE candidates are very used to showing their understanding of a literary text through a piece of creative extension or a recreative response. This can be both a very enjoyable and a very illuminating task at A level too.

Most Boards view the assessment of this kind of writing in a similar way to the assessment of a critical response, in that the skills and abilities being examined are the same as those which might be shown in a critical essay: response to themes, ideas, form, style, sub-text. But in a creative response the student has also had to identify consciously or unconsciously, to internalise and to recreate the way in which the author writes. This may take the form of pastiche or parody, but most students find the complex skills of parody more difficult than an attempt to imitate an author's approach and style. It is important that students can be made aware of how the author operates in order to be able to provide an imitation of the constituent elements. Some may be able to imitate the style without being able to imitate the structure, content and thematic development of the piece. Others, however, may be able to show their understanding of matters of content without being able to imitate the style. The most successful and accessible pieces of work of this kind at A level are often those which possess some of the strong and very particular features of the original. For this reason students find that the task of attempting an imitation of the content and style of Chaucer or Shakespeare, for example, very demanding in that it assumes mastery of uses of language from a period very different from today. A portrait of a pilgrim of their own from *The Canterbury Tales* will pose very detailed and sophisticated problems of syntax, vocabulary and uses of metre. Such a portrait in modern English prose, however, may be able to capture something of Chaucer's ironic style and may be able to capture an appropriate sequence of description and sub-text, but will be unlikely to be able to reproduce the particular tone and impact of the original without a very deep understanding of the original author's work. The attempt to treat the matter and style of a living author, however, may be more accessible for students as they will have greater awareness of the implications of the particular uses of language.

Some teachers have difficulty in achieving the balance in assessment between an understanding of the original author's work and the creative abilities of the student undertaking the task. It is clear that there needs to be an interplay between these aspects; the best pieces are likely to be those which capture the essence of the writer, as well as being artefacts in their own right.

Example 11

The first example is from a student who, having studied Larkin's poetry in *High Windows*, *The Whitsun Weddings* and *The Less Deceived*, is attempting to show her understanding of Larkin by creating three Larkinesque poems of her own. She notes the following in her description of the conditions surrounding the writing of this piece.

> Many of Philip Larkin's poems were discussed in class in small groups and as a whole class in detail. I studied some critics' view of Philip Larkin and tried to find a style in me like his.

Stasis

On shorter evenings,
Dark, frost and black,
Hides the sad
broken bodied ruins.
A bomb shrieks,
In the long deserted street,
its inevitable impact
splinters the remaining constructions.
It will be over soon,
It will be over soon –
And the children, who
are like frightened rabbits
Will find comfort,
they cannot understand
the reasons why:
But they laugh and play
In the ignorance of daylight.

THEY

The concrete jungle, they say,
A place where no one stops.
They scurry like rats,
Living off each other.

Their vehicles belch, thick,
black fumes pervade the air.
They, are impatient, hooting
and screeching, oh brother!

Suddenly a sea of grey overcoats
burst forth, from an opening underground.
Some shout at vehicles for hire,
others dart and dive for the shelter of other openings.

When the darkness comes, their
electric light abounds, false red and green
Invading the relief of the dark.
– You see, darkness hides ugliness –

Probably they, will not survive – NO STAMINA –
They, will not die young, of old age!
They, work too hard and eat too much,
They, smoke and drink to excess, Let's drink to them!

NATURE FOR NATURE'S SAKE

Pressed flowers,
Preserved for life,
Plucked from perfumed bowers,
but for them is this not strife?

Smothered between sheets of blotting paper,
they breathe no more.
But away from the elements, are they safe?
So what's the score?

Arranged on card or in brooches,
to give dramatic effect.
Art systematically encroaches
On nature that art should protect.

Several of Larkin's preoccupations can be identified in these poems.
There is a control of tone and atmosphere and in 'Stasis' the writer is
able to focus her imagery in the opening lines to create a convincing and
powerful mood, after the deceptively casual and low-key opening line.

The portentous nature of the repeated line in the middle of the poem leads into a more detailed and fully expanded image and, while the simile of the frightened rabbits is not particularly deep in its implications, all is gathered together in a thought-provoking and appropriate final two lines. The candidate's understanding of the way Larkin varies his registers is apparent by the interjection of 'oh brother!' in 'They', another poem where the form is carefully chosen. The Larkinesque characteristic of the surprise ending is captured here as is the use of everyday images and people's stereotypical response to them. The punctuation is less confident, in need of further revision, as is the metre. Perhaps the preoccupation of the writer was with content here. There are some effective images in 'Nature for Nature's Sake', a poem with a witty, provocative title. There is some depth of thought in this poem and again an attempt to capture different registers. The clumsiness of lines four and eight needs attention and the rather congealed syntax of the last two lines makes the thought more difficult to grasp than it might be.

There is a clear response in these pieces to Larkin. The student has understood crucial aspects of his thought, themes, content and poetic craft in a number of ways. She is able to organise her material in such a way as to reflect, at best, Larkin's modes of organisation. Her use of rhyme and rhythm is less assured than her understanding of mood and tone. 'Stasis' is the best, quite close to Larkin's 'Coming'.

Overall, the candidate shows a sound understanding of Larkin's subject matter, style and the development of ideas. She captures his changes of register and image and also conveys some of the dramatic quality of his poetry. She fulfils the grade indicators for the C grade and shows quite a sophisticated internalised understanding of some features of Larkin's style and content. There is a deliberateness and control in her own writing which perhaps puts this work just into the B grade with a mark of 10.

Some teachers, in order to try to make their students fully conscious of what they are attempting to do in a recreative piece, ask them to submit an analytical commentary, pointing to specific features of their work and evaluating their achievement. This can be informative in that such a commentary can point to an awareness which has not been produced in the piece itself and can therefore draw our attention to specific features of both works.

EXAMPLE 12

Task

The following piece was written after a study of James Joyce's *A Portrait of the Artist as a Young Man* and is accompanied by the student's own 'Critical Appreciation of my own piece of creative writing'.

– Goodbye, Stephen, goodbye
– Goodbye . . .

– Stephen, his Mother's voice echoed in his six cornered room and splintered his daydream. It was the sudden abruptness and severity of her voice, which immediately made him retrace the days' events; maybe she had discovered the empty biscuit tin, which he had 'emptied' several hours previously or even worse perhaps, she had discovered the remains of his father's best morningsuit, which Stephen had decided to cut 'down to size', as the two long bits at the back never had looked nice.

He felt a certain inevitability creep down his spine and contemplated whether to listen to his head and obey his mother's rather sinister call, or listen to his heart and slip into bed, pulling the covers over his head, shutting out all possible punishment. He decided the latter was unrealistic, taking into account his mother's present tone of voice and ran downstairs to find his mother beckonning him into the library, where his father had always told him off.

Sitting below the picture of some important ancestor, Mr Dedalus sat poised, ready for the kill and Stephen approached him; ready to be killed.

– Stephen, its about your schooling, his expression changed, You're in, my boy, Clongowes want you! They'll make a man out of you there . . .

Deaf to his father, singing praises of this 'school in the sky', he turned desperately to his mother for reassurance that his father was telling fibs – not that he was calling his father a fibber, but that they did not really want to send him to this Clongowesschool. Maybe, they had found out about his 'thieving' and his attempt at being the 'familytailor'; but his mother merely glowed with ecstacy at the thought of – her son being sent away from home. The mere thought of this, sent Stephen into near hysteria and the thought of beatings, rough and naughty boys, fights and playing cricket merely froze him to the spot. Surely his father had been joking when he spoke of his 'boisterous' school days, or had he . . .?

– . . . Stephen, Goodbye!

Critical Appreciation of my own piece of creative writing

The piece of work which I did based on James Joyce's *A Portrait of the Artist as a Young Man* I thoroughly enjoyed writing, however I am not sure if I did quite reach that same ultimate intimacy that Joyce illustrates in his book.

My main aim, which I tried to achieve in my piece of creative writing was in fact to overcome the hurdle of not just conveying, but also sharing those indepth emotions with my reader. I hoped to create this 'familiarity', primarily, by introducing an immediate lapse of time and by following it with a phrase or sentence, which would carry on the idea of depth: 'splintered his daydream'. I felt 'daydream' was an appropriate word to use here as it not only takes one back in to time, but it also suggests an exploitation of the person's mind, which is what I believe is James Joyce's secret.

I wanted to create an event, which had not been remotely portrayed in the novel, so that I could capture the readers imagination without him/her comparing it to any other incident in the book. I chose an 'incident' which I, myself, had experienced many times as a child: 'that certain inevitability' which I felt when I was summoned by a person of authority (usually my father!). However, I believe that this feeling is 'experienced' by every child and the immediate reaction is in fact to recall one's recent behaviour, bad or likewise. With this in mind, I chose, however, to express my feeling of 'horror' at my mother's 'ominous' call, after having recollected my recent behaviour, which could be regarded as 'unacceptable'. I did this because I felt that as the reader experienced their own emotions at my predicament; they could share these thoughts with my own feelings; instead of being able to have their own feelings on the matter.

I tried to keep as close to Joyce's own style of writing as I could, and I felt that an aspect of his work that I could not quite grasp, was the unique way in which he expressed his complete and utter dread with that of his fright. I hoped, primarily, to achieve this effect by creating a sinister atmosphere and surroundings: 'Sitting below the picture . . . ready to be killed'.

However, with hindsight, I can see that this was not enough; and the revealing of Stephen's deepest fears had to be illustrated in order to accomplish this effect on the reader.

Although, I enjoyed doing this piece of creative writing, I did feel that I did not achieve the same intimacy with the reader as Joyce did and I believed that the meaning of *The Portrait of the Artist as a Young Man* was in fact to overcome this aloofness between writer and reader and succeed in illuminating this 'aloofness'.

The original assessor of this piece clearly took on board the way such a piece of work can be used as an interim stage in the student's appreciation of the text by noting:

An interesting paradoxical conclusion which does indeed touch the nature of his style. Your reflections are revealing, and suggest ways of shaping your episode further towards Joyce.

The writer has been careful to provide an episode which could have come from this text. She concentrates, as does Joyce, on a very particular moment and describes it in detail with a consciously chosen and effective vocabulary. Stephen's age and stage of development are clarified for us during the piece, but as an integral part of the scene rather than as a piece of extraneous information. There is an attempt to provide both internal and external descriptions, although the register of these is not always wholeheartedly confident. In the commentary the writer points to Joyce's 'intimacy' and shows the very conscious way in which she has crafted one of the best parts of her own version. She shows good understanding of the effect Joyce's work has on a reader. She has combined her understanding of Joyce's subject matter, style, structure and point of view with her own experience and thus shows a fully engaged personal response to the original. She has begun to understand the psychological patterns in Joyce's own work and to recreate some of the ways in which these are conveyed. The illustrations are primarily in terms of vocabulary and consistency of tone, but the candidate's commentary shows awareness both of what she was attempting to do and of those places where she was not quite able to fulfil her intentions. This is a succinct, fresh and fully engaged piece of work which shows the critical and recreative skills appropriate to work of a B grade and a mark of 11.

9

CREATIVE WRITING

—

Several Boards have introduced as part of the examination requirements for coursework the option of freestanding creative writing. It is important that this remains part of an integrated course rather than as a freestanding 'creative' option whereby students include in their folder something they have written on their own. It may be that there are several adept and skilled writers doing the course who may indeed be equipped to include some of their own work, done for other purposes, in their folder. The majority of students at A level, however, can gain great benefit from undertaking their own writing within the structure of the course itself, as it allows them to internalise all kinds of aspects of writing which they are encountering elsewhere during their study of literature.

Perhaps the best strategy for preparing students for this part of a course is to link it to the texts being studied. Such matters as characterisation, form, structure, genre, register, tone, vocabulary and different aspects of development are all part of a study of literature at A level, and this is a way of trying to enable students to see the consciousness with which art is created, as well as to experience the trials, tribulations and joys of creation. Indeed, many students have chosen to continue to study English Literature at A level precisely because they so enjoyed their own personal writing at GCSE. Part of the study of and around a text chosen for coursework, therefore, will involve areas of creativity that students can then try for themselves. Discussion of student creations will inevitably lead to very engaged and critical classroom discussion and students will be enabled to see that part of the purpose of criticism is appreciation of how something has been created and the effects that it can have on different audiences.

If the course is arranged in terms of particular units of work, rather than as studies of discrete texts, creative work can begin by means of a creative response to a particular text (as outlined in the previous chapter) and then expand to the creation of students' own texts. Several Boards have developed assessment criteria for freestanding creative work and these vary to some degree, but common to them all are matters of communication, control and conscious organisation of form, ideas and expression. Some teachers are anxious about the assessment of this kind of work and yet feel little or no hesitation in criticising or assessing a printed work of literature. The process should be very similar, but the intention is rather different. The value of the assessment of freestanding creative work should be to point to the strengths and weaknesses of such a piece of work in order to alert the student to particular aspects of creation which they can then use to develop their powers. The three central areas of consideration in such an assessment are complexity, the ability to communicate and control over the chosen form.

Centres intending to offer students a creative writing option during an A level course would be well advised to ensure that the writing is contextualised properly and that students have access to the kind of help they have while studying texts. It is important, therefore, that they are made conscious of the conventions and possibilities of the form in which they are writing and are aware that the work they produce will be assessed. As always, it is vital that students have access to the assessment criteria so that they know how they are going to be assessed at the end. Workshops need to be provided where particular examples of finished work and work in progress are discussed, and where there is an opportunity to understand the nature and importance of revision, drafting and redrafting. The preparation and teaching of units of work which produce creative writing, therefore, need to be as careful and as thoughtfully structured as units devoted to the study of printed texts.

There are sometimes occasions when work which Moderators are given is clearly publishable (and, indeed, has sometimes already been published), even though readers may not agree exactly in the ways they describe the work.

EXAMPLE 13

The following student's poem appears to allow readers to construct various meanings from the poem while the poem itself adheres to a strict poetic form:

THE NONSENSE SYNDROME

Last night as I lay sleeping
Came a maiden to my bed.
When I asked her what she wanted,
This is what the maiden said.

'Polyp. Terrapin. Hosanna.
Dandelion. Mistletoe.
Lexicographer. Piano.
Taffeta. Geronimo.'

With these words the vision left me,
Pondering vainly at her gist.
Either what she said had meaning,
Or she was completely pissed.

Then again the next night came she
To the bedside where she lay,
And again in wonderment, I
Heard this lovely vision say:

'Gramophone. Suppository.
Elephant. Numismatist.
Amplifier. Plinth. Okapi.
Turnip. Psychoanalyst.'

Very worried now, I went to
Undergo psychiatry.
'Doc, at night this girl talks nonsense.'
His reply astounded me:

'Well, old chappy, vacuum cleaner.
Flying saucer. Halibut.
Windscreen wiper. Sock. Erection.
Whoopee cushion. Hazlenut.'

Sadly then I left the doctor.
Sadly walked along the road.
Waited at the bus stop for a
Bus to catch to my abode.

Soon I saw a bus approaching,
Crowded, dignified and red.
'One to London Road,' I ventured.
'Harpsichord,' the driver said.

Now I sit at home in silence.
Dare not venture out too far,
Lest I catch the nonsense syndrome.
Ventilator. Storage jar.

This poem adopts and sustains the regular stanzaic form and metre, although there are some very interesting and thought-provoking variations in the way the punctuation and individual lines are presented.

The registers and vocabulary are fascinatingly sustained, from the balladic, stylised syntax of the narrative, through the provocative lists of carefully chosen and sequenced items, to the voice of the persona. The poem is well-shaped, witty and thoroughly successful in engaging the reader's attention and interest. No words are wasted, each modulation in tone and register provoking appropriate responses on the part of the reader. Themes which emerge by implication from the sub-text and by attention to particular words are interestingly intertwined with a ballad narrative. In the view of the present writers, the poem is clearly publishable in its present form.

The following are some draft descriptions for the assessment of creative writing designed within the framework of AEB 660. (There is currently a pilot scheme operating for the assessment of creative writing using these draft descriptors. The descriptors will be modified in the light of the assessment of particular examples.) There are, perhaps, some problems in the wording of Bands 4 and 5 particularly, and reservations have been expressed about the highest level requiring 'mastery' (both as a sexist term and as something not appropriate for this level of work), but it is useful to try to apply these criteria as presently articulated. One reason for doing this is to suggest that the only workable criteria are not only those general enough to be derived from actual work, but also those specific enough to define levels of achievement. This may act as a reminder to readers that grade descriptors should be in a constant state of refinement and development if they are to reflect actual achievement year by year. The use of such descriptors is also a reminder that although internal marking and moderation relate to specific descriptors which are agreed upon, the final award of grades is by inspection by the Board's awarders. It is quite helpful, therefore, to be using different means of describing work within the same framework (in this case, within the same book).

Band 1

The beginnings of intention towards personal or creative engagement in writing may be discerned, but work at this level will be characterised by little ability to communicate intention, an absence of form or understanding of form, and lack of skill in the conventions of written presentation.

Band 2

Some modest attempt to compose the writing may be evident, and intentions will be at least partly communicated. Writing may be patchily successful, but without much sense of an appropriate holding form. Handling of writing conventions will vary from fair to weak.

Band 3

Expression will be comprehensible and will show a degree of competence in handling the chosen form. There will be evidence of an emerging personal perspective in the writing and intentions will be, on the whole, communicated. Handling of writing conventions will be fair.

Band 4

Writing will show competent handling of a chosen form, including clear communication of ideas, some flexibility in handling appropiate registers and a capacity to handle more complex areas of language such as 'sub-text', irony or rhetorical devices – even though these may be imperfectly treated.

Band 5

Work at this level will show skill in choosing and developing an appropriate holding form. Work will be clearly focused and contain interesting personal perspectives; it will be clearly communicated in an appropiate register, and will be well composed.

Band 6

Work at this level will show assurance in handling a chosen form; writing will be characterised by a willingness to engage in subtleties of meaning, as well as by clarity and power of expression; it will be characterised by elements of individuality and freshness, flexibility and adventurousness.

Band 7

Work at this level will show mastery of a chosen form, and a clear degree of creative or intellectual power in expression. Writing will be illuminated by individual wit and sensitivity; it will show a flexible command of a range of qualities such as subtleties, irony, metaphoric adventurousness and will be skilfully composed. Work in this category will range from very good to outstanding.

We can note that 'The Nonsense Syndrome' on p.91 followed a study of various ballads from different periods of English Literature, ranging from early ballads, through nonsense verse to modern ballads. Particular attention had been given during the course of work on poetry to the different ways in which poets use their form and metre to achieve specific and varying effects.

If we use these particular criteria for creative writing for 660 we can describe the poem in the following way. It shows mastery of the chosen form and uses it for the specific purposes of introducing different voices and styles to engage the reader's interest and to enable the reader to differentiate quickly between the different tones. A clear degree of creative and intellectual power of expression is shown, both in the consistently archaic expression of the narrative sections and in the extremely well-chosen and provocative single word lists. There is clear wit and a keen awareness of the ways in which poets can encourage readers to construct meanings. There is a wide range of subtle effects created in a short and succinct frame. There is irony and adventurousness in the impact of the chosen words. The poet achieves complexity of effect, particularly in the seventh stanza and in the relationship of the material in the second, fifth and seven stanzas to the metaphorical impact of the last line of the poem. It can clearly be seen that the poem fully exhibits all the criteria for Band 7 of the assessment criteria and that it therefore merits full marks available for creative writing in these terms (15 for AEB 660), denoting the highest mark in the A grade.

EXAMPLE 14

The next example is of a piece of work deriving from a study of Noel Coward's *Blithe Spirit*. While embarking on a piece intended for the previous category in the syllabus (Creative Extension), the candidate decided that she wished to write her own play rather than write in Coward's style. Although the piece began as a pastiche of Coward, the final version below shows few of Coward's characteristics and has become, through its stages of revision, the candidate's own attempt to use dramatic form.

Task

Creative writing, undertaken after a reading of Blithe Spirit.

TIME TO KILL – A COMEDY

Place: purgatory – a sitting room – Earth.
Time – present.

Scene 1

Curtain rises – stage in two halves – one well-lit has dry ice everywhere, a white iron bench and a desk with a computer and a man with a halo sitting at it. The other half is dimly lit. It shows a sitting room with a man sitting with head in hands. The man NIGEL is dressed in black tie but looking a mess.

PHOEBE enters stage left with dry ice. She is in her early thirties, she is smartly dressed, attractive and looks rather lost.

PHOEBE: Where the hell am I?

ANGEL: (*looks up, answers with a kind of indifference*) Take this. (*hands her a piece of paper from printer*) It's your serial number.

PHOEBE: I don't want a list of numbers, I want to know where I am, and why does my head hurt?

ANGEL: (*Without looking up*) You've just died but you have to wait here a couple of years.

PHOEBE: Yer right and my name's Donald Duck.

ANGEL: (*looks up*) According to this your name's Phoebe Smith.

PHOEBE: Smythe.

ANGEL: Oh no, not another one.

PHOEBE: Don't blame me, blame my husband.

ANGEL: Go and sit down please. (*Sits on bench woman in white tunic with a halo rises up on stage*)

PHOEBE: You must be an angel!

WOMAN: No – I had a coronary during the school nativity play.

PHOEBE: How awful!

WOMAN: Mmm, play was ruined. (*Opens packet of cigarettes offers one to Phoebe*)

PHOEBE: No thanks, I don't, you only live once.

WOMAN: (*looks at PHOEBE*) Oh dear, not quite hit you yet has it dear. You are dead (*pause*) you cannot die again – cigarette? (*Offers her one*)

PHOEBE: Don't mind if I do. (*lights cigarette*) I knew I was going to die you know.

WOMAN: Really, how was that dear?

PHOEBE: The brakes of my convertible didn't work. (*ANGEL gets out loudspeaker*)

ANGEL: Mrs Smythe, please report to the reception area. (*PHOEBE walks over*)

ANGEL: You're lucky, small waiting list due to increase in atheism and price of cigarettes, only two years to wait.

PHOEBE: (*horrified*) 2 years? 2 years for what?

ANGEL: In purgatory of course.

PHOEBE: Well what am I supposed to do?

ANGEL: God knows, but he is unavailable at the moment, sorry. (*He returns to his work*) (*PHOEBE returns to the bench*)

PHOEBE: What am I to do, death is so boring.

WOMAN: You could watch earth.

PHOEBE: What?

WOMAN: You are sitting in front of the viewing screen, you can watch anything.

PHOEBE: Good heavens – or should I say purgatories. (*she laughs*)

WOMAN: You obviously had a real shock dear. Look, I'll set the screen and you can watch your home if you like.

PHOEBE: I don't know. I would have to see my husband suffering so much, shattered by my death, unable to face life. Poor, poor man, if only he knew. It would be interesting I suppose (*pause*) OK, set the screen. (*Woman presses buttons on back wall then goes back through trap door*) (*lights rise gradually on other half of stage. NIGEL still head in hands*)

PHOEBE: Oh poor Nigel, how he suffers! (*lights rise more on sitting room*)

NIGEL: (*looks up*) Christ, what a hangover! (*croaky voice*) Darling, fetch me some Alka seltzer. (*Puts head back in hands*) Oh . . . (*groans*) (*Door opens. MELODY enters stage right. She is dressed in short skirt, stilettos and cropped top, basically an obvious bimbo*)

MELODY: (*handing glass*) Here you go sweetiepie. Would you like a massage?

NIGEL: No, and will you keep your voice down.

MELODY: (*whispers*) Sorry baby. (*Silence on that part of the stage. MELODY sits next to NIGEL, picks up a magazine and flicks through it*)

PHOEBE: What is going on here? Melody in my house, the secretary with my husband. She's probably using my bathroom, washing her peroxide hair in my shower, spilling her red nail varnish on my carpet – Aah – I can't stand it, I have to do something . . .

MELODY: Feeling better honeybun?

NIGEL: No.

MELODY: Poor baby, at least you have me to look after you. I'll be the best wife in the whole world sweetness.

PHOEBE: Wife – it's worse than I thought.

MELODY: I'd like lots of children, wouldn't that be super, hmm lovely?

PHOEBE: Children! I have to put a stop to this – pauvre Nigel. (*She moves over to the ANGEL's desk. MELODY continues to talk to NIGEL but we cannot hear her*)

PHOEBE: Ahem (*coughs. ANGEL looks up, rather annoyed*)

ANGEL: Yes?

PHOEBE: I was wondering if, well, I mean, is it possible to send someone up here.

ANGEL: I doubt it.

PHOEBE: Oh, when is Melody Brown due to die then?

ANGEL: (*sighs*) Hold on (*taps on computer*). Melody Daffodil Brown – death 3rd November 2042.

PHOEBE: Damn. (*pause*) couldn't you move it forward to like today?

ANGEL: Mrs Smythe, I do not accept requests, I am an angel and I do wish people would respect me. (*stands up, looks serious*) I spent 2000 years getting here, ok it's not much you may think. A receptionist so what (*rather upset now*) you are thinking, aren't you? It has good prospects ok? One day I may even be (*He lifts head in pride*) a member of 'Gabriel's Gang.' My life's not perfect you know, people think civil servants have it all but we don't, worst of all (*pause*) I can't even touch type (*he sits down, very upset*)

PHOEBE: Oh – sorry – 'bye then. (*Moves back to bench. Woman flies down next to her*)

WOMAN: Hello dear, how's life – sorry, bad choice of words.

PHOEBE: Awful – my husband's been tricked into marriage by a mouth on wheels.

WOMAN: Oh – well, you could kill her.

PHOEBE: (*laughing*) Yer right. 'The Night of the Living Dead II!'

WOMAN: I'm being serious. Listen, you now know death is fine, it's nothing – by the same reasoning then murder is nothing.

PHOEBE: I suppose so, but how do I go about it?

WOMAN: Well, there's the old struck by lightning or freak yachting accident, or car crash? cliched but effective – oops – no offense meant there.

PHOEBE: None taken. So how do I change the weather?

WOMAN: Easy – I work part time in the weather centre – anything you need – just ask me.

PHOEBE: Let's think – lightning – hyperthermia, I know black ice!

WOMAN: Coming up, or down (*flies up off stage*). (*light rise on – other stage*) (*MELODY rises, gives NIGEL kiss on cheek*)

MELODY: Just going down to the chemist – must buy some more finger nails.

NIGEL: OK, watch the weather, quite icy, wouldn't want you to slip would we now. (*they laugh*)

MELODY: Oh, your so sweet, bysee bye then. (*Walks off with her 'suitable' shoes*)

PHOEBE: Get ready . . .

(*Blackout on stage. Traffic sounds, sound of high heeled shoes walking down a street – slip – loud scream from woman – first few bars of Chopin's funeral march – dies out*)

End of Scene

This play shows some understanding of the conventions of dramatic form. The setting is established by description, the speakers are clearly identified, there are stage directions which indicate both the way some of the speeches are to be spoken and what kind of staging is required. The candidate has given much freedom to a designer in not specifying much beyond the general effect to be produced. The play begins with an attempt to engage the audience's interest by not specifying too quickly where Phoebe is. This anticipation, however, is not sustained very long, and we quickly learn that she is in purgatory. There is some attempt to characterise the different speakers by the language they use and there is a clear (if rather predictable) narrative sequence which the audience can follow quite easily on a split stage. Events occur quickly. There is no indication what might happen after this 'Scene I' is over and in some ways the candidate has produced a small sketch. There are many fillers in the dialogue which become rather repetitive and need more stylistic variety to engage interest fully. Limitations in reproducing speech fitting to the different characters, and the unsophisticated nature of the humour which tends to arise not from character but from the desire of the author to amuse, show insecurity in the use of the form. The writer can occasionally plant information which is picked up later, but some crucial details (like the coronary during the nativity play) are provided as mere information and not developed thematically or dramatically. The expression is generally competent (despite some uncertainty about register and conventions of annotation), and the dramatic form is sustained even though the dramatic impact is uneven. The writer has had a clear idea of her basic plot structure for this particular scene although she has not allowed many themes to emerge either implicitly (one is not sure about the significance of the nativity play) or explicitly. There are one or two moments where the waiting in purgatory is communicated to the audience, but events happen too quickly for this to be sustained or developed in a conscious way. The reader ends the piece not really knowing whether this is a consciously wrought introduction to a play which is to be developed or whether it is an unfinished fragment. Some indication of the writer's intention in producing this piece on its own as a finished item would clearly have helped to contextualise it. In terms of the descriptors for this syllabus, the candidate's achievement lies at the upper end of Band 1, deserving a mark of 4.

10
THE REST OF THE COURSEWORK

—

The AEB minimum requirements are eight pieces of work. We have already discussed the six items based on an individual text, but what about the remaining two pieces?

Pieces 7 and 8 can be anything, and we have already looked at some of the possibilities available in our discussion of creative writing. Some centres have used these two slots as preparation for the Extended Essay, as they allow students to develop strategies of coping with more than one text at a time. However, they can also provide an opportunity for widening the student's course still further, since they are the place where students can include work which is centred on a theme or genre but which is not specifically related to one text.

If one is thinking of minimum requirements, then pieces 7 and 8 can consist of extra work on the six chosen coursework texts, work on examination texts, pieces of practical criticism or other creative items. But there is also a chance to use these slots to enable students to show off the whole range of their work, or to include work they are proud of but which otherwise does not have an obvious place in the folder. Some candidates have submitted different kinds of published work here. Sometimes students have prepared analyses of the organisation and execution of performances. Others have submitted an individual report on a group task. A few centres have included various kinds of linguistic work which has been integral to the course but which has been skills rather than text-based. Very occasionally, Moderators have seen pieces which reflect analytically on the processes of group learning and group talk. Given the climate of change at the moment, these pieces are particularly useful to teachers who are seeing ways of building up an A level course onto the top of the National Curriculum.

These pieces, therefore, can reflect the whole course and the individual's experience of that course, rather than just the individual texts which have been studied. Those centres which have taken seriously the idea that there needs to be a formal gathering together of what has been achieved by the students as individuals and as a group during the course, have encouraged students to undertake a critical evaluation of their learning process to include as one of these pieces. Those centres offering AS level with the same group have sometimes encouraged all their students to include their own critical reading log here.

Pieces 7 and 8, therefore, can be a stimulus to teachers to think again about the course as a whole and to encourage reflection. The example given on p.106 is of this kind – a student applying knowledge of the different kinds of critical apparatus which have been encountered during the course with a personal eye. This is sometimes the place for the most lively, personal and engaged writing, but it is also in the experience of Moderators sometimes the dullest part of the folder, where students appear not to have internalised their learning as fully as they might have done and have simply fished among their 'rejected' essays for those with the remaining highest marks. It is sometimes disappointing to see that pieces 7 and 8 have gained the lowest marks in the folder rather than the highest.

The assembly of the final completed folder can be a very useful way of sharing, discussing and evaluating what has been learned during the coursework. The final folder is the student's own achievement and should reflect the balance, range and depth of the student's experience of literature and personal development during the course. In this way, students who are selecting their best pieces of work and re-reading them to choose which of the many pieces they have written during the two years best reflect their achievement, can gain a real sense of self-esteem. They will be able to identify what they have become confident at doing and will be able to isolate specific areas of skills which they need to concentrate on during their revision for the examined half of the course.

It is desirable during this final selection procedure for students to own both their achievements and their shortcomings in order to remind them that the learning they have undertaken has been done, and can continue to be done, only by them. It is not the teacher's course; it has been and is theirs. The process of final selection allows them to return to the Aims and Assessment Objectives of the course and to prompt them to make selections which show off the range and depth of their work to its fullest advantage. Thus the final selection process needs to be validated by the teacher and by the group and can give rise to some very useful discussions and agenda-setting for the remaining part of the course.

The first example of work comes from a student with a particular interest, but one which he did not pursue for his Extended Essay. It is his own title, but refined and formulated in discussion with the teacher.

Example 15

Task

Detective Fiction – The Book-Cover Guide to Pleasure

The student noted on his cover sheet: 'Time allowed 5 weeks. Largely independent reading and writing. Six novels read in preparation time as well as previous detective fiction reading experience.'

Part I

My versions of book-cover 'tasters' for P.D. James's *Shroud for a Nightingale* and Dashiel Hammett's *Red Harvest*.

Part II

I have used my two new book-cover write-ups to stimulate a discussion of the pleasure I received in reading the two novels in terms of:

1 Literary Pleasure
2 Escapism
3 Knowing the Formulae
4 Solving a Puzzle
5 Seeing Justice Done
6 An Easy Read

Part III

A short conclusion summarising my preference.

Part I

Shroud for a Nightingale
By P.D.James

> There was a squeal, high-pitched, horribly inhuman, and Nurse Pearce precipitated herself from the bed as if propelled by an irresistible force. One second she was lying, immobile, propped against her mound of pillows, the next she was out of bed, teetering forward on arched feet in a parody of a ballet dancer, and clutching ineffectually at the air . . .

So begins the horrific tale of murder and manipulation in the gloomy precincts of the Nightingale Training College. But it is not until the second death within the same claustrophobic surrounds that Chief Superintendent Dagleish arrives to unravel the web of intrigue and malice that binds the terrified residents of Nightingale House. But perhaps one of them has nothing to fear.

Pit your wits against those of Dagleish to bring justice in the deceptively sincere world of Sisters, surgeons and student nurses. At least one of them is a murderer and many more may hold the key to unlocking the mystery. Unrivalled in its ingenuity, pace and originallity, the new 'Queen of Crime' will keep you on the edge of your seat with this un-put-down-able book.

Red Harvest
By Dashiell Hammett

> When he first heard Personville called Poisonville he thought it was due to the speaker's accent. Once he'd been to the town he knew differently.

Asked to 'clean up the town' by the father of his murdered client, the Continental Op tries to do just that by ruthlessly playing-off the four gangs against each other. It becomes more than a job – a personal obsession. He'll only be satisfied once the gamblers, liquor pushers, blackmailers and murderers that lead the four territorial gangs that control the town (Max Thaler, Pete the Finn, Lew Yard and Noonan) are no more. But as the Op explains '. . . There's no use taking anybody into court, no matter what you've got on them. They own the court, and besides, the courts are too slow for us now.'

This fast-moving thriller set in the gangs' hideouts and the back-allies of an American town plagued with vice and corruption, emmerses you in a blood-bath of switching loyalties and deceit, not least from the Continental Op himself.

Part II

1 Literary Pleasure
The style and language chosen to tell the story plays an important part in giving of pleasure when part of the whole package. P. D. James is respected for her move away from the plain narrative style so distinctive in classical English detective novels by Christie or Wentworth. I enjoyed reading her use of imagery (c.f. Part I) – 'teetering on arched feet in a parody of a ballet dancer,' – because it gave the book more life and made the action a lot more vivid. Often, a reader who has turned to P.D. James after, say, Christie, is frustrated at her efforts to closely describe events with a creative flourish, but I found it refreshing.

The pleasure I received from Hammett's style was due to the exposure to a different culture reflected in the language. This ties in with escapism, for although it lacks the poetic flare of Chandler, it did enable me to savour the alien culture that it represented. However, I soon took this for granted.

2 Escapism
The claustrophobic, sinister setting of *Shroud for a Nightingale* is a familiar scenario and exploits my expectations of a closed household in which the murderer is at large. However, the sense of escapism is minimised because

it is so familiar and the setting relatively ordinary. Escapism is escaping into a different world, and the hard-boiled American novel lends itself a lot better to my personal escapist needs because it is so far removed. There is a romanticism connected with gangsters that is lacking from the world of nursing and I want to vicariously experience the latter world because it is unfamiliar and can be exciting within the security of a book. This is my main source of pleasure from Hammett and the least important in the pleasure I gain from James. My unwillingness to submerge myself in the routine of a nursing-home means that it is infact easily 'put-downable' compared to the sustained interest evoked by Hammett's more enlivened world.

3 Formulae
The recurrence of Adam Dalgleish in James' book exploits my expectations in that I think I know what sort of investigation is to ensue. P. D. James works fairly religiously within the expected framework of a classical English detective novel using confined surroundings, timeless investigation, and then a final clue that leads to the drawn-out explanation, usually by the Detective but sometimes by the murderer. She keeps to this pattern in *Shroud for a Nightingale*, and instead of manipulating my expectations by guiding my response, it frustrated me. The endless interviews that even Christie didn't drag-out so long, bored me. Hammett begins within the true 'hard-boiled' tradition when Continental Op's client is murdered before he reaches the town, but the brutality of the Op and lack of a conclusive ending flew in its face. It was a relief from Chandler's step-by-step investigation but ultimately meant the narrative was disorganised and a pattern was undetectable. Mini-climaxes left no sting at the end, and the entire book's lack of structure was disappointing. Writing to a traditional formula could have solved this.

4 Solving the puzzle
A strong sense of puzzle solving pervades James' work, and to say 'All is revealed in a conclusion unrivalled in its ingenuity, pace and originallity' would be accurate in the context of any of her novels. I enjoy attempting to solve the mystery but actually feel cheated if I actually succeed. At the same time, I resented the introduction of an unavailable fact at the end of *Shroud for a Nightingale*, and there is a scence in which both author and reader must play by the rule. The high drama of the denouement partly made up for my resentment at the flaunting of the rules on her side. I believe it is the desire to solve the puzzle and the consequent revalation when the author proves he or she can dream up an even less feasible solution that is the source of the pleasure. A pattern should be discerned at this point, and this complete lack of pattern in *Red Harvest* made it a lot less satisfying to finish. The solution to the initial murder came well before half-way through the book, the narrative exploiting into a confused state of gang-warfare.

5   *Seeing Justice Done*

Shroud for a Nightingale is a perfect example of the world being put right in a detective novel, unlike *Red Harvest* which totally debases the principle. James' murderer rides the world of a blackmailer and an unpopular student and is then killed himself by the focus of her crime, an ex-Nazi war criminal. Real justice comes when the Nazi war criminal commits suicide. This purging goes even further when a fire destroys Nightingale House. Miss Beale, Inspector of Nurse Training Schools who opened the book, re-visits the centre at the very end of the book to see the demolition of what she sees as '. . . a horrible house; an evil house'. This cyclical narrative is complete and satisfying compared to the utter lack of achievement at the end of *Red Harvest* resulting from the death of the four gang leaders. There is no client to be satisfied, no justice was really done, and the Op proved himself to be corrupt and unworthy of the trust I'd put in him at the beginning as the inforcer of law and order. The removal of one of the main threats left me wondering why I first endured a savage catalogue of distruction.

6   *An Easy Read?*

In the questionnaire we issued to people who enjoyed reading detective fiction, an overwhelmingly popular answer to why they enjoy detective-fiction was that it was easy to read. P. D. James can be hard-going sometimes, and I tended to skim over any psychological or philosophical content because it's not what I wanted to see. I expected a storyline with clues and little more when I read my first James. It took a zeal away from the book which Hammett contained. James' book was lethargic except at the beginning and end, while Hammett's thriller was sustained action. It urged you to read on. The monotony of Dalgleish's investigations that made up the meat of *Shroud for a Nightingale* did not make it easy to read in comparison to the welcoming perpetual motion of *Red Harvest*.

Part III: Preference

Without doubt the security of identifying a formula, the literary style and the satisfaction and the revelation of the denouement meant I enjoyed *Shroud for a Nightingale* a lot more than what I saw as an unstructured and more superficial account of gang-warfare. At first I enjoyed the exposure to a new literary culture, but without the fascination of an ongoing plot I soon lost interest and found it tedious.

Escapism is, I think, the most basic of all reading pleasures, as many of the other pleasures depend on it. For example, puzzle solving is often dependent on feeling part of the book's world and the search for justice stems from half-regarding the characters as real people as well as what could be seen as a sociological or psychological desire for good to conquor bad. Therefore the pleasure comes when escapism meets other important underlying factors with interlocking purposes which one often sub-consciously expects.

The student has generated his own form for producing this piece and has made an interesting attempt to match his own preconceptions with some of the novels he has encountered. It is a method that whets the appetite and (rather in the mode of detective fiction itself) makes the reader want to find out what the writer thinks. The categories are thoughtfully chosen and the identification in the passages in terms of the six items is careful and worthwhile. The writer is confident about his approach to the genre and is clear both about the features of detective fiction and about his own response to the genre, despite his assuming more familiarity with the content of these novels than the reader might always have. The reference to the group study consisting of the questionnaire is valuable and suggests a successful way of creating an individual outcome from group activities. It is sometimes a little disappointing that the student makes such fleeting reference to other works he has read; a little more detail and analysis would have enhanced the study. It would have been interesting to discover how much his findings on the basis of these two novels would have had to be modified in the light of his extensive reading experience. It is, however, a thoughtful and individual piece of work with some interesting observations about style and structure and some confidence in the ability to analyse features of texts. The work hovers between the C and B grades. A mark of 9½ would be appropriate.

EXAMPLE 16

This example, produced towards the end of the course, stems from the candidate's frustrations with her course. It contains a nice mixture of knowledge and scepticism which particularly appealed to the present writers.

Task

My Experience of English Literature and A Critical Appreciation of Baa Baa Black Sheep.

i) STUDENT'S DECLARED AIMS AND PURPOSE OF THE ESSAY

I wrote the first essay a day or so after the mock English exams. I wanted to explain why I wasn't satisfied with the A level English course so far. While trying to revise for the mock I'd read a previous paper and it had an article by Judith Sproxton about how students are trained to be spoonfed and expect the teacher to know what's right. The last question on this article was to say about your experience of English Lit. I had loads to say on this and really hoped we'd have the same paper for the exam. We didn't so I spent a day writing this and an essay on Time that I wasn't too keen on doing. I handed this essay in and found that quite a lot of people agreed with me. After I had my mock results back (they weren't too good) my teacher suggested writing a parody of the exam or writing something for myself rather than writing what I thought the examiner wanted. So I wrote a critical appreciation of Baa Baa Black Sheep. I tried to use all the terminology everyone thinks they should use like 'alliteration' and 'juxtaposition' and tried to make it as pretentious as possible.

I've been trying to work out for a while now why I haven't been enjoying English. I've always liked reading and in the fourth and fifth years it was one of my favourite lessons, I never considered not taking English as an 'A' level. So why do I hate writing essays and find writing them so difficult? I have now come to a conclusion about this partly after reading an extract of an article by Judith Sproxon in the 1988 Paper 1. This said exactly what I was feeling.

I feel like a fake when writing some essays because I think that the title is asking for specific things which the teacher has already told us sometimes directly, sometimes indirectly. By indirectly, I mean through pointing us to certain pieces of text and leading a 'discussion' where they ask certain questions to which they expect certain answers so we come away feeling that we have thought for ourselves and worked out our own interpretation of the text, when in fact we have taken on the teacher's understanding of this text. I therefore, with some essays more than others, have come to see English as reading a text, taking on the teacher's interpretation and ideas, receiving an essay title which is looking for certain points which we have already been told, writing these points and then getting a good mark which will help me get my 'A' level.

I have been trying to define English Literature as a subject for myself and have tried to work out why I took it in the first place and what I'm getting out of it (apart from an 'A' level). I haven't come to a conclusion to any of these points except perhaps the decision that I'm not getting anything out of it. I can't see any point in doing the subject if it doesn't interest me because surely interest in a subject has to be the main reason for doing it. I don't want to feel that I'm doing a subject just to get a qualification in order to prove that I'm better than someone else who hasn't got that qualification. I think that one of the problems with all my 'A' level subjects is that is they are unavoidably geared towards the exam. We end up learning things not because they are of any personal interest or will help us to gain a greater understanding in life but because the examiners look for this, because we know it pleases them. I sometimes wonder when I get a good mark for an essay if this is because I said what the teacher wanted to hear, so someone who got a lower mark may have actually written a 'better' essay where they had formed their own opinions. This brings forward the question of the whole education system. It is so geared towards results that people end up working not for any personal gain but to prove themselves in front of the others. This leads me to look at the mark first and then read the comment, this leads us to compare results and immediately think someone is better or cleverer because they got a higher mark.

The English Lit. syllabus seems to leave no room for personal response, the exam papers in particular. There seems to be no role at all for creative work or working out your own ideas which the text may have stimulated. I think this is because the whole syllabus has evolved from a narrow definition of English Literature as a subject. I think there are two ways of using a text. The first involves looking at how the ideas are expressed rather than what the ideas are; so in effect looking at what you can see rather than what the author is saying. I feel that this is the case with English, particularly in the exam where you are expected to examine bits of text in detail and talk about technique, 'distinctive qualities', 'main features' and so on. The second way of using a text, which for me is of more use, is to use the text as a starter for your own ideas. A text usually provokes certain responses and leads to certain emotions, so surely it would be more productive to chart these? I think that through this you can show that you have understood a text. Some essay titles kill anything that the text has made me feel. I think that writers must write primarily to sort out their own feelings and to share them with other people. I think therefore that any ideas which we get from the writing, any way it starts us thinking should be recorded.

I find it a false exercise to look at a piece of writing to see how it is written because I never go any further than that. I can look at a poem and say 'oh it's got a rhyming couplet' or 'there's 10 syllables to a line' but this doesn't have any meaning for me. I tend to think so what if it has. I can't see any reason for this form, so writing this seems to be a waste of time. I see this as a passive exercise because although it involves some thinking, you are only writing about what you can see. It also seems to be pointless if it has no meaning to me. I think that if I can see some meaning in the poem why should I write about rhyming couplets? This form of writing seems to me like a game of Hide and Seek aimed at satisfying the examiner rather than the student. The examiner sees things 'hidden' in a text so they give us a clue to help find it – the question – and reward us if we do say there's a rhyming couplet or whatever. I can't see the point in essays which just seem to be an elaborate way of asking for a re-hash of the text. I think there should be room in the subject for creative writing. In other arts subjects this is the case – in art you draw; in music you compose – so why not write when studying English Lit? I think it may also lead to a greater understanding and appreciation of literature.

I think the way we study literature leads to a passionless understanding. If I read other people's essays I find them boring (mine included) because they are all basically the same. We feel we must keep to a certain technique – people say you can't write 'doesn't, 'you've got to say 'does not' and although we've been told it's ok to use 'I' by one teacher, I still feel wary about using it as if 'me' shouldn't enter into it. And I wonder if I can be funny or sarcastic but come to the conclusion that it's an English essay so you've got to be serious because after all it is a serious subject. Perhaps I put these restrictions on myself but I do feel as if I've got to conform to a written style. I think however that the only thing you can get from a book is the effect it has on you so surely an essay should be written in your own style.

Going back to the article by Judith Sproxon, I read it and felt really enthusiastic about what she was saying. I then looked at the first question and lost all interest. 'What are the main points which Judith Sproxon is making about students' attitudes to literature when at university?' It seems like a more sophisticated version of the reading comprehensions we used to do in junior school. It also has nothing to do with the article. It seems to be an example of exactly what Judith Sproxon is criticising.

I enjoyed writing this and found that it flowed, something unusual for me. I have come to expect to have problems writing essays, to dread them and spend hours hoping for inspiration which I have yet to find. But I've begun to think well why shouldn't I enjoy them? Writing this had made me realise that I need to feel something for what I'm writing and if I don't it becomes a dry, boring, pointless exercise.

ii) BAA BAA BLACK SHEEP

Baa baa, black sheep,
   Have you any wool?
Yes sir, yes sir,
   Three bags full;
One for the master,
   And one for the dame,
And one for the little boy
   Who lives down the lane.

On a first reading the poem seems nonsensical and leaves many questions unanswered – who or what does the sheep represent? Who are the master, dame and little boy? What is the significance of the lane? Does the fact that the sheep is black hold the key to the meaning of the poem? One needs to formulate answers to these questions to give some meaning to the poem and one must also take into consideration the language as well as the written style.

The words 'Baa baa' used by the poet can have two meanings. There is the obvious imitation of the supposed sound a sheep makes but the poet could be seen to be using a pun here playing on the fact that 'baa' can sound like 'bah'. This gives the poem a whole new slant for the word 'bah' is usually used in a derogatory manner. This could indicate that the 'sir' of the poem is oppressing the sheep. The sheep is nothing to the 'sir' but a source of income. He therefore has no respect for the aforementioned sheep and exercises his power over it by speaking to it in a disparaging fashion.

The words 'Baa baa' seem to be spoken in a sarcastic perhaps bitter tone.

The 'sir' seems to be mocking the sheep by speaking its language. It appears that the poet is emphasising the utter futility of being able to say 'Baa baa' if one can obtain no profit from it. This brings into view the theory that the sheep is possibly old or has been a bad worker (or producer of wool) in the past. Perhaps the 'sir' has fallen onto hard times and needs the sheep's wool in order to survive. It seems to the reader that the sheep is the 'sir's' last resort on which he must now rely. Perhaps he doesn't relish this role and this is what leads him to speak to the sheep with such contempt.

The poet uses alliteration in the first line of the poem, 'Baa baa, black sheep' which helps emphasise the sarcasm of the speaker. One is forced to spit the words out in an aggressive way.

The next line, 'Have you any wool' could be read in different ways. The 'sir' could be speaking aggressively and it could therefore sound abusive. Another reading which may be more effective in giving a meaning to the poem could be to give it pleading tone leading to the idea of forthcoming industrialisation. The 'sir' (or the sheep) must provide enough wool for the master, dame and little boy as quickly as possible for he is aware of the threat industrialisation poses to him. Unless he delivers the wool quickly his customers will discover the new factories where wool is spun in seconds by infallible machines which replace unreliable people. The poem effectively juxtaposes the idealistic picture of rurality with the threat of coming urbanisation.

So who are the master, dame and little boy? One might presume that the master is a landowner to whom the 'sir' must pay taxes perhaps in the form of wool. The dame could be the master's wife or possibly an 'old dame', another derogatory term for women. The character of the little boy is interesting for why should he want wool, how would he be able to afford it and why doesn't he have any family? One possible theory perhaps fantastical, could be that the little boy is a version of the modern-day rent-boy. Why else would the 'sir' be so anxious to give him wool but as a form of payment even blackmail to keep the little boy quiet.

The poem therefore has many underlying themes which only becomes apparent on detailed study. Although it appears to be an innocent little verse at a first reading, one can see that there is a lot of valid social comment in it which is as significant to our modern society as to the society which it describes.

The first of this candidate's two pieces is strongly personal, interesting and provocative. It attempts to deal with what the student feels to be the purpose of criticism both in general and for her specifically. It concentrates on the processes of reading and criticism, and concludes effectively with a realisation (which seems fresh) that learning needs to be personal. The candidate appears to be rather uncertain when addressing 'Baa Baa Black Sheep' about what is illuminating and what is 'as pretentious as possible'; it is this nice interplay between making and satirising critical comment that gives the piece its complexity, for without some sophistication of critical equipment the candidate would not be in the position to satirise the process of criticism. It is particularly interesting that the candidate here achieves critical realisations just when she thinks she is satirising. There are, however, some very effective and amusing passages in a piece which the writer enjoyed constructing and the reader enjoys reading. It demonstrates the ability to reflect and analyse and also to structure and control a personal response. It merits an A grade and a mark of 13.

At the present time the AEB is developing draft descriptors for whole folder assessment, so that in time it may be that marks are arrived at by assessing the folder as a whole rather than by the present method of aggregating the marks for the individual components. It will be worthwhile and interesting development work in the next few years to see what differences these two methods of assessment produce and whether the whole folder assessment will lead to a more or a less accurate overall result. The following descriptors appear in early draft form and are being piloted at the time of writing (1991):

Band 1

Folder work may contain the rudiments of knowledge and ideas, though response is likely to remain at a basic narrative level. Folders may be patchy or incomplete. Better work will be comprehensible even when there is evidence of poor or inaccurate expression.

Band 2

Folders within this range will show some acquaintance with the texts, with some attempt made to move beyond narrative treatment. Work overall may show modest degrees of engagement with the ideas of texts, as well as some knowledge and understanding. Topics may be handled implicitly rather than explicitly at this level, and there may be unevenness of attainment throughout the folder.

Band 3

Folder work will show a fair grasp of texts at a narrative level, and show some capacity to handle ideas. Textual references may be incomplete; more relating of texts to topics may be needed, but writing should provide evidence of some success in reading and reflection, expressed in a basic framework of argument. Candidates may, in places, provide evidence of more attentive engagement with texts, even though treatment will still require more substance, or better organisation.

Band 4

Folders in this range will show reasonably sound knowledge of texts and evidence of attempts to present a view. Understanding of texts will be evident; expression will usually be clear, even when it could be more carefully organised and better focused. Some emerging competence may be revealed in linking texts to topics, and in composing coherent frameworks of assessment. Overall, folders will show evidence that some balance, variety and range in writing tasks has been achieved, although work may reveal uncritical dependence on, rather than active interpretation of classroom handling of texts.

Band 5

Folders in this range will reveal careful, well-engaged work, characterised by good textual awareness and a willingness to handle related ideas. Folders will be soundly organised and substantial, and go beyond a mere recitation of received ideas on texts and topics. While some assignments may lack individual critical edge, candidates in this range will show skill in building on ideas and evidence, and reveal that they are capable of developing and maintaining different kinds of reflective writing and critical argument. Overall, there will be clear evidence of success in achieving balance and range in completing a variety of writing tasks, and a corresponding emergence of awareness of different authorial voices in texts.

Band 6

Folders will provide evidence of accomplished well-written work which covers areas with thoroughness and skill. Work may reveal individual flair and include some of the qualities to be found in the highest mark range. Even in parts where critical engagement and handling of ideas may not be entirely assured, there will be clear evidence of comprehensive understanding of texts and topics, profitable reflection, discrimination, and a capacity for sustained argument. Folders will be successful in achieving a good blend of variety, range and balance in writing tasks, and a capacity to draw ideas together with clarity and some subtlety.

Band 7

Folders at this level will show coherent, fluent organisation of material and of ideas. Accurate textual awareness, individual exploration and sharp insight, will be revealed. The writing will be adventurous, thorough and succinct. Folders will show skill in making free use of texts to achieve effective connections of ideas and themes. An individual 'voice', confident, sensitive and thoughtful, will be evident throughout the folder. There is likely to be a considerable range of achievement within these marks, from very good to outstanding. The top rating should be given where the overall blend of range, variety and balance in writing is judged to be of exemplary quality. Such a folder will not only be especially well composed and thorough, but will also contain insights or approaches that surprise and delight the reader.

11

CONCLUSION

—

This book has been put together during a time of considerable uncertainty about the nature of post-16 education, and the possible effects of change on A level. The rhetoric from ministers is about the 'gold standard', 'excellence', the folly of tampering with something which is 'working well'. And yet those of us closer to it know that any problems of match and transition which we had between O levels and traditional A levels are nothing compared to the difficulties of match and transition from GCSE into an A level which has made no attempt to change.

What has been said in preceding chapters about the selection of texts, the setting of assignments, the need for variety, range and balance in the folders finally produced, the emphasis on student autonomy and individual development within the structure of the course is, in our view, entirely compatible with building on the demands of the higher levels of the National Curriculum for English. The government now seems, however, to have temporarily abandoned its proposal that core skills of communication, problem solving, personal skills, numeracy, information technology and modern language competence should be included in the study programmes of all students post 16, whether they are following vocational or academic courses. This proposal need not have alarmed teachers of AEB 660. Throughout this book we have emphasised the importance of the development of subject specific skills. The AS or A level course can provide relevant contexts for exercising them, without distorting the overall purpose of studying literature.

The features of AEB 660 which have attracted teachers from the beginning: the coursework component, the 'open book' examinations and the invitations to experiment and develop new ways of encouraging students' responses to literature and to assessing them make this A level examination flexible enough to cope with most changes imposed from outside. More importantly, these features of the AEB 660 syllabus also encourage teachers to keep their courses and their own practice under review and to see change and development as an important part of their A level teaching.

BIBLIOGRAPHY

Advancing A Levels (HMSO, 1988).

A Level English: Pressures for Change (NATE Publications, 1990).

Batsleer, Davies, O'Rourke, ed., *Rewriting English* (Methuen New Accents, 1985).

Berger, J. *Ways of Seeing.*

Brown, J. and Dixon, J. *Responses to Literature – What is being Assessed?* (Schools Council Publications, 1984).

Brown, J. and Gifford, T. *Teaching A Level English Literature: a student centred approach* (Routledge and Kegan Paul, 1989).

Dixon, J. *English 16-19: the role of English and Communication* (Macmillan Education, 1979).

English A Level in Practice (NATE Publications, 1988).

Gifford, T. 'Writing about drama in performance for Literature coursework' *(English in Education* 21, no. 1, 1987).

Goddard, R. 'Beyond the literary heritage: meeting the needs in English at 16-19' *(English in Education* 19, no. 2, 1985).

Greenwell, B. (ed.) *Alternatives at English A Level* (NATE Publications, 1988).

Hackman, S. and Marshall, B. *Re-reading Literature,* (Hodder and Stoughton, 1990).

Knight, R. (ed.) *English in Practice: Literature at A Level* (Scottish Academic Press, 1989).

Lee, V. J., ed., *English Literature in Schools* (Open University Press, 1987).

Marking Procedures in English at Advanced Level (Associated Examining Board, 1988).

Ogborn, J. 'Teaching A Level: a two year plan' *(English Magazine* 12, 1984).

Peim, N. 'Redefining A Level' *(English Magazine* 17, 1986).

Protherough, R. (ed.) *Teaching Literature for Examinations* (Open University Press, 1986).

Scott, P. *Reconstructing 'A' Level English* (Open University Press, 1989).

West, A. 'The Limits of a Discourse' *(English Magazine* 18, 1987).

Widdowson, ed., *Re-reading English* (Methuen New Accents, 1982).